King of Hearts

King of Hearts

Drag Kings in the American South

BAKER A. ROGERS

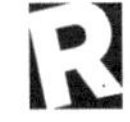

Rutgers University Press
New Brunswick, Camden, and Newark, New Jersey, and London

Library of Congress Cataloging-in-Publication Data

Names: Rogers, Baker A., author.
Title: King of hearts : drag kings in the American South / Baker A. Rogers.
Description: New Brunswick : Rutgers University Press, 2021. |
Includes bibliographical references and index.
Identifiers: LCCN 2021006634 | ISBN 9781978820531 (paperback) |
ISBN 9781978820548 (cloth) | ISBN 9781978820555 (epub) |
ISBN 9781978820562 (mobi) | ISBN 9781978820579 (pdf)
Subjects: LCSH: Male impersonators—Southern States—History. |
Gender expression—Southern States.
Classification: LCC PN2071.I47 R63 2021 | DDC 792.02/8—dc23
LC record available at https://lccn.loc.gov/2021006634

A British Cataloging-in-Publication record for this book is available
from the British Library.

∞ The paper used in this publication meets the requirements of the American National Standard for Information Sciences—Permanence of Paper for Printed Library Materials, ANSI Z39.48-1992.

www.rutgersuniversitypress.org

Manufactured in the United States of America

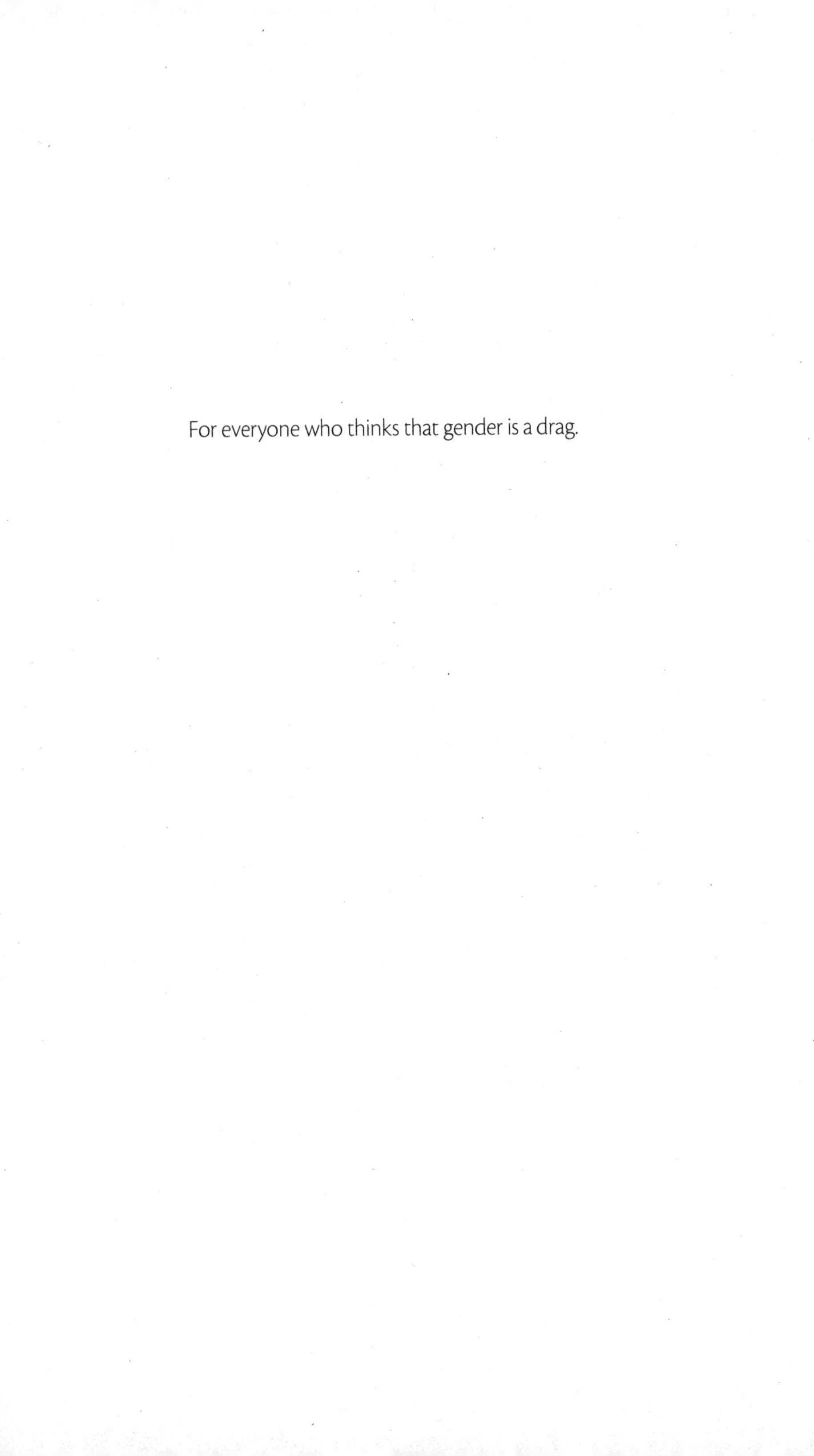

For everyone who thinks that gender is a drag.

Contents

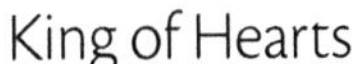

King of Hearts

Introduction

The lights are dim, everyone is laughing and having a good time, the music is so loud you can barely hear yourself think, and the smell of booze is so strong it cancels out the sweat and odor of the decaying bar. I'm up next, and the emcee announces, "Please welcome to the stage, Macon Love!" The crowd cheers as the first chords of *Don't Stop Believin'* blare through the speakers. I walk onto the stage with my blonde mullet wig flowing behind me and a confidence that seems to come from some other place. I lip-synch the lyrics, "Just a small-town girl, living in a lonely world, she took the midnight train, going anywhere." The crowd roars and holds up dollar bills as I move across the stage. Women start to make their way to the stage to get my attention and give me money. The thrill of the experience is overwhelming and unexplainable. For a few moments, I am transformed to a white man in an eighties hair band. After the song, I make my way to the bar for another drink and to flirt with my fans. The women's attention creates a feeling of pride and sureness. In those few hours of the drag show all of us kings try to *hold on to that feeling*—the feeling of indescribable comfort in our own skin, the feeling of confidence and power that men are taught to have but those of us socialized as women all too often lack.

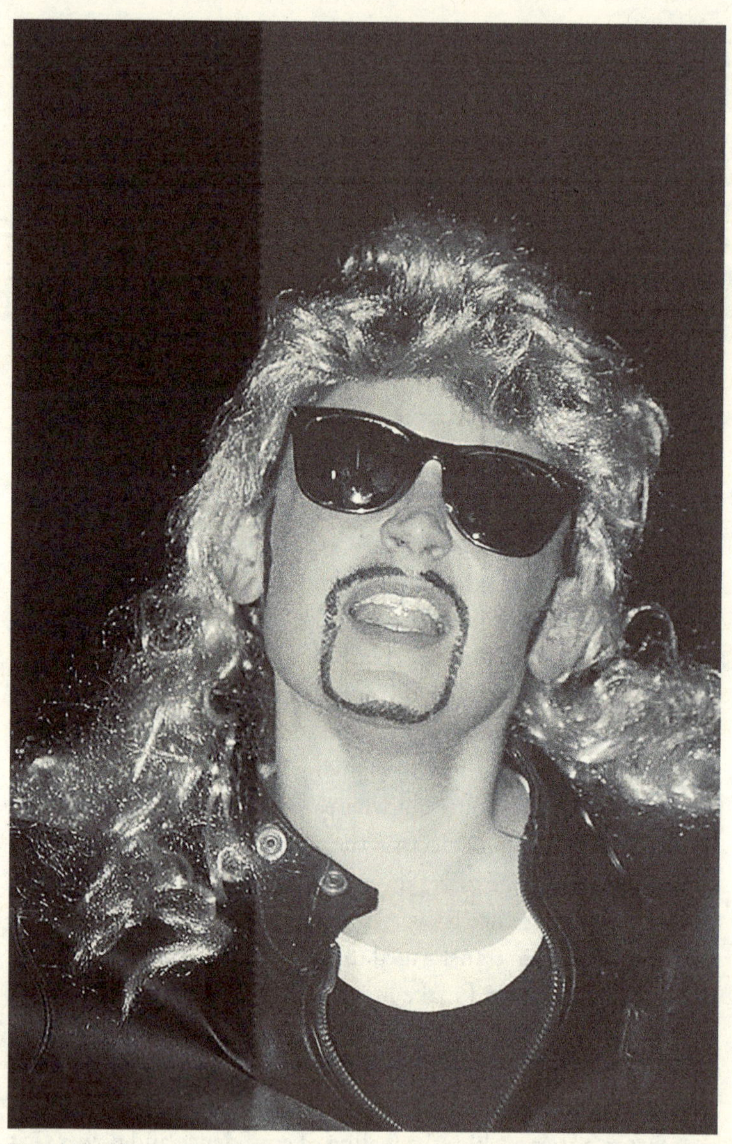

Drag king Macon Love sings in a blonde mullet and dark sunglasses.

Who Is a Drag King, and What Do Drag Kings Do?

Unlike drag queens, drag kings have not achieved broad cultural penetration—there is no basic cable drag king show with millions of viewers. So, by way of definition, drag kings are people—regardless of sex or gender identity—who perform masculinities in the context of a drag show or contest (Baker and Kelly 2016). While women have performed as men in various settings throughout history, drag kinging did not become common in the United States until the 1990s (Halberstam 1998; Shapiro 2007). The easiest way to describe a drag king to people with no cultural references is that drag kings are "the opposite of drag queens." However, this description leaves a lot to be desired.

My goals for this book are to introduce readers to the exciting world of drag kinging, to demonstrate its unique importance in the southeastern United States, and to discuss the sociological implications of this type of performance. But, first, let me explain a little more about what drag kinging is for those who may be unfamiliar with this type of performance. Most drag king and queen performances, at least in the Southeast, take place in a queer bar or at Pride events—events celebrating lesbian, gay, bisexual, transgender,[1] and queer[2] people, identities, civil rights, and pride.

Performing as a drag *king* involves presenting your body and attire as masculine, usually exaggeratedly so, and lip synching to songs (usually) by male artists. To get ready for a drag show, kings often spend weeks or months picking out songs, making and preparing costumes, and practicing their performances. Most drag shows, other than daytime events at Pride festivals, occur late at night in bars or clubs. A typical show in the Southeast begins around 10 P.M., although they rarely start on time. Kings arrive

1. Transgender, or trans, is any gender identity that does not align with the cultural expectations of the sex a person was assigned at birth.

2. "Queer" is used in this book to refer to individuals who identify with nonnormative genders and sexualities; it replaces concepts like "LGBTQIA+" (which stands for lesbian, gay, bisexual, trans, queer, intersex, and ally, plus), in order to be as inclusive as possible.

much earlier to get ready for the show, often in a cramped, hot, tiny dressing room off of the stage area in the bar. These "dressing rooms" are really closets at the back of the bar, because most bars were not built for the purpose of drag performances. Inside these small, cramped spaces, the atmosphere is usually jovial and upbeat.

On the night of the performance, the initial step for many drag kings is taping down their breasts. This process has changed some over the last decade that I have been doing drag, as the drag king performers in the Southeast have shifted from largely cisgender[3] lesbian women to more of a mixture of cisgender lesbian women, gender nonbinary[4] people, and trans men. Still, any king with breasts will likely tape them down to achieve the flatness of a man's chest. Some kings wear binders,[5] others use Ace bandages, but the majority of southeastern kings with breasts continue to use duct tape to bind. As my dad always told me, "You can fix anything with duct tape and WD-40."

Taping down your breasts can be done in two ways. Duct tape can be wound around the body multiple times, pulling in your chest as much as possible. If this method is used, some plastic wrap should be wound around your body under the tape to prevent the duct tape from sticking to sensitive skin. The other method of binding breasts with duct tape is to tape each breast to the side by putting the tape over your nipple and pulling the tape as tight as possible to the side. While the first method hurts a little less, the second method allows kings with breasts to show their chest in performances without the tape showing.

After taping down their breasts, some kings then pack their underwear to appear to have a penis bulge. For kings without a

3. Cisgender, or cis, refers to a person's gender identity aligning with the sex they were assigned at birth (i.e., a person assigned female at birth who identifies as a woman, or a person assigned male at birth who identifies as a man).

4. Nonbinary is a gender identity that falls outside of the binary categories of man or woman; people who identify as nonbinary may or may not also identify as trans. There are numerous nonbinary gender identities, including, but not limited to, genderqueer, agender, two-spirit, etc.

5. Binders are compression undergarments used to make your chest appear as flat as possible.

"package" themselves, one can be approximated by stuffing socks in their underwear or using a dildo or a specific packing device. Then a drag king does their facial hair and makeup. For kings who do not have facial hair already, applying false facial hair is usually important to pull off the illusion of drag. Some kings use makeup to draw on a mustache and/or beard, while others use actual hair. When I performed, I was taught to use spirit gum[6] to glue my own hair to my face. You take some of your own hair clippings, cut them up finely, put the spirit gum on your face where you want your facial hair, then use a makeup brush or a fine paintbrush to apply the hair to the glue. In addition to adding facial hair, some kings also use makeup on their face and bodies to give themselves a more masculine appearance. For instance, filling in your eyebrows can make you look more masculine; shadowing your chest and abs makes you look more muscular. When I performed, I also often wore mascara, like many of the eighties hair band members.

Next comes the costume. Costumes vary widely and can be a contentious subject among kings. Some kings spend a lot of money and time preparing specific outfits for every single performance. Others wear masculine clothing they had in their closet. For instance, some of the younger, less experienced kings in this study reported wearing "street clothes" to perform, particularly if they preferred more "butch" clothing in their offstage lives. Many of the more experienced performers highly objected to this practice, arguing that unless a performer was willing to make a significant effort with their appearance, the performance was not drag. For instance, Rider Oliver Fox, a twenty-five-year-old white straight person who identified his gender as mentally male, explained his position on costuming: "It's gotta have rhinestones on it or I won't wear it. . . . You've just got to have some awesomeness to it. Rainbows or sparkles or, absolutely no jeans, absolutely no jeans. Closet drag is terrible. I'm so sick of it." The more lavishly costumed performers, like Rider Oliver

6. Spirit gum is a type of glue that is, at least nominally, safe for your skin and usually sold at costuming stores.

Fox, contend that drag kings who wear street clothes are "lazy" and an embarrassment to drag kinging.

Thus, many more experienced kings in my study considered fashion and costume guidance to be a critical part of mentoring less experienced kings. Tex, a sixty-six-year-old white butch gay woman, discussed how younger, less experienced kings did not want to spend money on outfits, attributing this to laziness. While more experienced kings often complained about casually dressed kings, these less experienced kings were often using drag as a resource to help transition their gender identity to man and their gender expression to masculinities outside of drag. Therefore, many of these performers were more interested in showcasing "everyday" masculinities that would translate to their offstage identities if, or when, they came out as a man and/or male. Additionally, the relatively low socioeconomic status of most of the kings I interviewed made elaborate costuming impractical. Costuming is extremely expensive and time-consuming, and only a few of the kings I spoke to make this money back through performing. Therefore, for some drag kings, buying and making elaborate costumes was not an option.

Once a king is taped, packed, made up, and dressed, they head to the stage for their performance. Kings in my study usually selected upbeat, fast-paced songs for their performances, explaining that it was more difficult to maintain their masculine personas during slow numbers. Kings reported that for audiences composed primarily of women, "sexier" songs brought greater tips from audience members as well. Some kings modeled their drag persona after another man, usually a famous performer such as Prince, Aaron Carter, or Michael Jackson. Others based their drag king image on another version of themselves, for example, what they thought they would be like if they were men, or at least the most boisterous parts of their personality. Rider Oliver Fox referred to putting the more lurid parts of his personality on stage as letting his "freak flag fly." Justin Case, a thirty-five-year-old white gay woman, said, "I find the most confident, energetic, fun-loving part of my character, I just take that and exemplify it and times it by five and then I put that out there and that's what Justin Case is."

Costumes may be designed to impersonate those of the original artists singing the song a king is performing, or they may just be in the style of the type of music performed. Some kings' personas are stable, regardless of song choice, and others alter their drag personas for each song. In addition to performing gender on stage, kings usually also perform sexuality. Some kings perform as gay men (desiring men), and others perform as heterosexual men (desiring women), but the sexual identity of the performer may not necessarily match that of the king's persona. The sexuality of the king might stay static across performances or may change depending on the song or act they are performing. This is different from queening, where masculine or lesbian women identities are rarely, if ever, performed.

Drag has many benefits for those who perform. First, drag is fun. Drag is entertainment. A performer gets on stage, lip-synchs and dances, and entertains a group of people who are there to see them. As a form of entertainment, a few kings have made lucrative careers out of drag. For instance, the most well-known drag king in the Southeast who has made a career of drag kinging and male impersonation is Spikey Van Dykey out of Florida. More popular kings often have promoters or bookers like other types of performers; they get scheduled at shows across the region or even the country; and they make money from booking fees and tips at shows. Still, making a living at drag kinging is very rare, especially in the Southeast. I know of only a few kings who have succeeded at this. In this study, the two oldest kings, Tex, a sixty-six-year-old white gay butch female in South Carolina, and Patrick Jacquard, a fifty-eight-year-old white lesbian female in Tennessee, were the only two kings who had made a living performing drag and working with other drag kings. Nevertheless, they were not able to survive only on performing, so both kings had other careers as well. While Tex was performing drag around the world, his primary career was as a professional wrestler, and later he owned a gym. Patrick Jacquard opened a number of gay bars in the Southeast and now works as a drag promotor, in addition to performing himself.

More importantly, in addition to being fun and earning them money, drag is liberating for many kings. The first time I taped

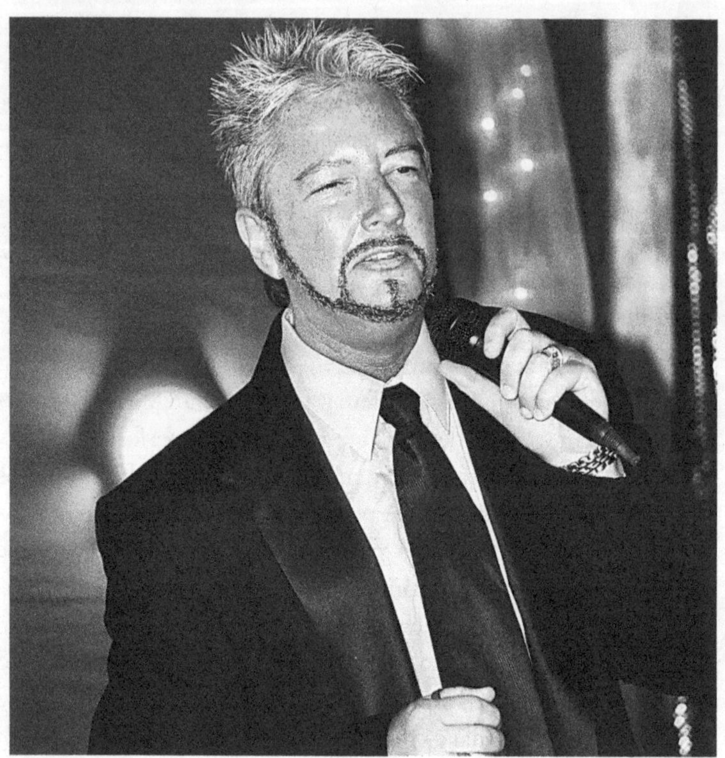

Drag king Patrick Jacquard sings into a mic in a black suit and tie.

down my breasts and put on facial hair, I stood in the mirror and stared at myself. It just felt right. I felt freed from my breasts, which have bothered me my whole life, and I felt empowered to walk out in front of a room of strangers and be me—or at least a freer version of me, Macon Love. It is this liberating aspect of drag and its importance in the southeastern United States that I focus on in this book.

The Basics: Sex, Gender, and Sexuality

While the concepts of "sex," "gender," and "sexuality" are highly interconnected, the distinctions between these concepts are important and necessary for understanding drag. Sex refers to biological characteristics, such as genitalia, hormones, and chromosomes, used to assign people to a category of male, female, or intersex at birth. Gender is often, but not always, related to sex. Gender is the social expectations of how a person acts, usually based on the sex they were assigned at birth. Gender can be broken down into identity—how people think of themselves in terms of gender (man, woman, trans, genderqueer, etc.)—and expression—how people perform masculinities, femininities, or androgyny in interaction with others. Gender identity and expression are not naturally occurring facts; rather, they are taught and enforced by society. Whether or not people agree with or follow the expectations of gender, they are always held accountable to acting in a way that aligns with their assumed sex (West and Zimmerman 1987, 2009).

To appreciate drag kinging, it is necessary to understand gender expression or performance, especially the performance of masculinities. Masculinities are performances. Masculinities refer to more than merely being male bodied or having a specific personality type (R. Connell 2005; Pascoe and Bridges 2016). Masculinities are socially constructed, varied, and "inherently relational"—that is, masculinities always exist in relation to femininities and other forms of masculinities (R. Connell 2005, 68; C. Friend 2009). What masculinities have in common is their ability to "reproduce subordination of women to men, and some men to others" (Sumerau 2012, 462).

Finally, sexuality refers to attraction, both sexual and romantic. Sexuality does not automatically align with expectations based on a person's sex or gender. One may be sexually attracted to the same sex or gender (lesbian, gay, queer, etc.), romantically attracted to a different sex or gender (heteroromantic), or not attracted to anyone sexually (asexual) or romantically (aromantic). The list of possible sexualities and combinations of sex/gender/sexuality is endless.

In this book, I focus both on how gender is performed by kings in and out of drag. That is, this book is most concerned with gender performances and identities. However, because sex and sexuality are so highly related, they will also be discussed. Overall, most of the kings I spoke with were not immersed in academic jargon and viewed their gender identities as a personal reality rather than a political statement. Many of the kings in this study identified their gender as trans or nonbinary, and they clearly differentiated trans identities from other nonbinary identities, such as genderqueer, non–gender specific, gender fluid, and so forth.

The Southern United States

The southern United States intersects in a variety of ways with kings' identities and makes drag kinging unique in this area of the country. Place is always crucial to understanding gender and sexualities (Abelson 2019; Brown-Saracino 2018; Carter and Borch 2005; C. Johnson, Gilley, and Gray 2016; Reed 1986, 2008, 2018). Specially, the southeastern United States is a distinct geographic location, both in reality and in the national imagination (Abelson 2019; Friend 2009; Friend and Glover 2004; Reed 1986, 2018). This region, especially in rural areas, is known for stereotypical gender norms (Carter and Borch 2005) and conservative political and social views concerning gender, race, and religion, which play a central role in the understanding and experiences of all Southerners. My desire is not so much to explain why the South is not like the rest of the United States, but rather to explain why drag kinging in the South is the way it is (Cobb 2005).

Like most geographic locations in a globalized world, it is difficult to define the exact boundaries of the region. Depending on who you ask, what is considered "the South" can vary widely. Reed (2018), a well-known sociologist of the South, argues that the most reliable definition of the South is "where people believe they are in the South." Defining the South as places where the majority of people believe they are in the South and identify as Southerners demonstrates that the boundaries of the region are murky at best and do not necessarily fall along state lines. But due to the subjectivity of this definition, and its difficulty as a research measurement, most scholars rely upon state borders to draw the boundaries of the region. There are thirteen states in the United

States where the majority of people say they are in the South; no other states meet this qualification (Reed 2018). These states include the eleven ex-Confederate states (South Carolina, Mississippi, Florida, Alabama, Georgia, Louisiana, Texas, Arkansas, North Carolina, Virginia, and Tennessee), as well as Kentucky and Oklahoma (Reed 1986, 2018). This is the definition of the Southeast I use for this project.

Like all geographical regions, the southern United States "is a site of contradictions," but E. Johnson (2008, 1) argues that race, and specifically the institution of slavery, makes the South's contradictions even more complex. The horrific legacy of slavery still haunts the South today, as southern institutions and culture were founded on the free, forced labor of African slaves (Cobb 2005; E. Johnson 2008, 1). Contradictorily, Southerners are often known for being good-mannered and caring people (E. Johnson 2008). These images of the South are often hard to align. Yet, despite these contradictions, many people continue to claim southern identities and use the region to define themselves and others.

Southerners across various cultures and ideologies continue to feel a sense of loyalty to the region and continue to desire that the South strive for a distinctive culture that is set apart from other regions of the country (Reed 2018). Likewise, Southerners, more than other Americans, think of place "possessively, as *theirs*" and prefer the South to other locations (Reed 2018, 33). Historically, Black Southerners were "denied their regional identities" as Southerners (Cobb 2005, 262). Based on the injustices Black people faced in the South and on causes such as Black pride movements that focus on the African homeland, most people assumed that Black people would not even want to identify with a southern regional identity. This is why Cobb (2005, 262) states, "Perhaps no phenomenon of the post-civil rights era is more striking than the readiness, even eagerness, of African Americans both in the South and outside it to identify themselves unequivocally as southerners and claim the region as home." The majority of people in the United States today agree with Southerners that this region is distinct, and that Southerners are different from people in other regions of the country (Reed 2018). For instance, Southerners are assumed to be more courteous, more religious, more conservative, more loyal to family, and more content with life than people from other regions of the United States (Reed 1986, 2018).

Much of the uniqueness of southern culture is connected to the higher rates of political and social conservatism, which are strongly associated with religion. As other regions of the country seem to be converging culturally due to globalization and mass media, the South continues to remain distinct, especially in terms of religion and politics. In fact, in some ways the South is moving away from the national norm (Reed 2008). This trend seems to have accelerated under the Trump administration, which made it once again acceptable to be openly racist, sexist, homophobic, and so on (GLAAD 2020).

The majority of Southerners continue to strive to preserve a culture where men are dominant and where "traditional gender-roles" remain intact (Carter and Borch 2005). While this often reinforces negative stereotypes about Southerners held in other regions of the country, such as being patriarchal and intolerant (Carter and Borch 2005), many Southerners have come to see these insults as a badge of honor that demonstrates their commitment to religion and conservative politics. While Black and white Southerners have had extremely different histories in this region, conservative religion and issues of morality, such as abortion and homosexuality, have served as a uniting force between conservative Black and white people in the South (Cobb 2005). As Cobb (2005, 289) explains, "Black southerners did more than their share to sustain the South's reputation as the 'Bible Belt.'"

Despite change and diversity in the South, it appears that it will remain a distinct region of the United States, at least for the foreseeable future (Reed 2018). Many Southerners strongly identify with the region and feel they have a stake in ensuring its continued distinction from other areas of the U.S. (Reed 2018). Cobb (2005, 336–337) eloquently summarizes the uniqueness of the region: "For all the contemporary statistical data documenting regional convergence and the physical evidence afforded by skyscrapers, suburban sprawl, and gridlocked expressways, I have yet to encounter anyone who has moved into or out of the South and did not sense that, for better or for worse, living here was different from living in other parts of the country." Despite the shortcomings of the region, most Southerners love where they live and have a strong attachment to their community and history (Reed 2018). Unfortunately for queer Southerners, the downfalls of the region, especially conservative politics and religion, are amplified in many ways.

Queer Southerners

The religious and political conservatism of the southern United States increases prejudice, discrimination, and oppression against queer people, especially trans, nonbinary, and bi+[7] individuals (Barton 2012; Baunach, Burgess, and Muse 2010; Bradford et al. 2013; Mathers, Sumerau, and Cragun 2018). As one of the kings in this study, Roscoe McCoy, a forty-five-year-old multiracial pansexual gender fluid person living in Georgia, described it: "There's such an overwhelming Evangelical presence here . . . that has stunted our [queer] community. . . . I think that in the South, finding [queer] culture has been harder because of . . . that conservativism and the Evangelicalism, which is very puritanical in thoughts about sexual identity, gender identity, gender roles, and judging that."

Even though states within the United States must adhere to changing federal legislation regarding queer rights, the backlash against the expanding rights of queer citizens and the implementation of reactive policies such as "religious freedom" bills make the relationships between conservative religion, conservative politics, and prejudice and discrimination extremely clear. These reactive laws and policies indicate that many conservative Christians in the South continue to place their conservative beliefs above their relationships with queer people (Rogers 2019).

7. Bi+ refers to sexual identities that are not monosexual (attracted to only one gender/sex), including bisexual, pansexual, queer, polysexual, demisexual, polysexual, fluid, etc.

Historically (and some would argue even still today), Southerners did not openly oppose or even discuss queerness in public. As long as queer people did not "flaunt" their queerness or their queerness did not threaten what Southerners felt was "right," then most queer people were left alone to live their lives in private (Daniel 1996; E. Johnson 2008). This is why I often tell people, "In the South, I'm read as straight and cisgender until proven otherwise." Southerners, like members of many other subcultures, want to believe you are like them, but once you show you are not, negative actions may follow. Shifting federal politics have also led many Southerners to feel threatened and under attack, leading them to seek out queer Southerners to confront and harass, rather than let them live quietly in their midst. For instance, some southern Christians feel that they are under attack, and may even be arrested for speaking publicly about their opposition to homosexuality (see Rogers 2019 for examples).

While some cisgender gay men and cisgender lesbian women have started to gain some acceptance in the South, even in certain religious subcultures, this acceptance is often based on the continued marginalization of others who are believed to pose a greater threat to the status quo, such as transgender, gender nonbinary, and bisexual people (Cragun and Sumerau 2015; McQueeney 2009; Sumerau and Cragun 2018; Sumerau, Grollman, and Cragun 2018). Primarily, cis lesbian women and cis gay men who are willing to uphold certain traditional ideals about gender (e.g., that gender is binary) and family (e.g., that families are heterosexual and patriarchal) are beginning to gain some acceptance in the region. For example, some Christian groups in the South are beginning to accept cis lesbian women *if* they are married, monogamous, and raise their children in ways that the church deems acceptable. Same-sex marriage allows cis gay men and lesbian women the ability to imitate heterosexuality and monogamy. As someone in a same-sex marriage, I am not arguing that same-sex marriage is bad per se. Rather, I am arguing that same-sex marriage allows some queers to gain acceptance while further ostracizing those who cannot fit into this heterosexist institution.

Geographic location has been left out of intersectional studies for far too long. Most research on queer lives, in particular drag, has been conducted in "urban enclaves" like San Francisco and New York (Stone 2018). The lack of research in the South and other rural areas has led to a metronormative narrative of queer life that leads society to view all queer life through the lens of cis, white, urban, upper-middle-class, gay men (Stone 2018). Despite the problems for queer people in the South, over a third of queer people in the United States live in the South (Stone 2018). Although the focus on queer life is often centered in big cities on the East and West coasts in the United States, queer life also prospers in the South, in rural areas, and in "ordinary cities" (Brown-Saracino 2018; C. Johnson, Gilley, and Gray 2016; E. Johnson 2008; Kazyak 2012; Stone 2018). This reality of where queer people live shows that the metronormative image of queer life excludes most queer people in the United States (E. Johnson 2008; Stone 2018).

Queer people choose to stay in the South for many of the same reasons other people do, including work, family, cultural loyalty, inability to move due to socioeconomic status, and even an affirming gay community or chosen family (E. Johnson 2008). While most people in the United States assume they understand the South, and rural areas more generally, their imaginations of these regions are usually quite limited and stereotypical. As such, many people assume that queer people choose to leave the South and rural areas for urban enclaves as soon as possible (Kazyak 2012). On the contrary, many queer people choose to stay in the South and rural areas. Often queer people find these areas comfortable, or at least it is where they feel most at home (Abelson 2019; Kazyak 2012). Further, just as southern identity is important to many Southerners, it is also important to many queer Southerners. Queer Southerners often perform "southernness," such as being polite, saying "yes ma'am" and "no sir," speaking with a southern drawl, or identifying as religious, in order to gain acceptance through likeness and to portray that they belong (E. Johnson 2008, 2; Rogers 2020). So, who are these queer people who decide to live in the South? Where do they find resources and community? And most importantly for this book, how does drag help these queer people carry out their lives in the South?

By ignoring queer Southerners, society has perpetuated the notion that the South is uniformly closed-minded and conservative—religiously, politically, and socially (C. Johnson, Gilley, and Gray 2016). Nevertheless, as E. Johnson (2008, 3) explains, queer lives in the South "necessitate a reconsideration of the South as 'backward' and 'repressive,' when clearly gay community-building and desire emerge simultaneously within and against southern culture." Moreover, the idea that the South will not or cannot change is detrimental for many reasons. First, it ignores the region's immense diversity and the progressive people here struggling for equality. Second, and more importantly, it leaves queer people in the South without the resources necessary to survive and thrive. For example, state legislatures continue to promote and pass bills aimed at denying trans people access to medical care and public facilities (e.g., bathrooms and locker rooms), limiting workplace protections for queer people, and blocking access to accurate identity documentation for queer people (e.g., birth certificates and driver's licenses) (Freedom for All Americans 2019).

Meet the Kings

The majority of participants in my study (72 percent) identified their sexuality as monosexual (lesbian, gay, or heterosexual/straight). This cohort of southern drag kings is thus unique among the studies that show that trans and nonbinary individuals are generally more likely than cisgender people to identify as bi+, or beyond binary classification (Galupo et al. 2014). While only nineteen of the sixty kings identified as cis, forty-four identified as monosexual.

In what follows I provide a brief introduction to each king, using their own terms for their various identities. Because I am using their own terms, sometimes identities may be confusing to the reader; however, it is important to describe respondents the way they see themselves. For instance, Shook ByNature described himself as a thirty-five-year-old African American androgynous

Kings' Identities

NUMBER OF KINGS	60
Gender Identity	
Female[1]	19
Male[2]	10
Transgender[3]	18
Gender Nonbinary[4]	13
Sexual Identity	
Lesbian	24
Bi+[5]	17
Heterosexual/Straight[6]	15
Gay	4
Race/Ethnicity	
White	42
Black	5
Multiracial	5
Native American	2
Hispanic	3
Pacific Islander	1
Jewish	1
Mexican	1
Location by State	
South Carolina	32
Tennessee	9
Georgia	8
North Carolina	5
Arkansas	2
Kentucky	2
Mississippi	1
Florida	1

1. All of whom were cisgender.
2. All of whom were transgender.
3. Including transgender, FTM (female-to-male), trans male, trans man, transvestite, and mentally male.
4. Including androgynous, androgynous metrostud (this respondent stated that he passed for either male or female), stem (a combination of stud—sometimes referred to as butch/masculine—and femme), gender fluid, gender neutral, genderqueer, nonconforming, non–gender specific, girly/stud, and unisex.
5. Including 3 kings who identified as bisexual, 6 as pansexual, 6 as queer, and 1 as open.
6. All of whom were transgender.

metrostud lesbian in North Carolina. He described what he meant by androgynous metrostud lesbian in detail. Shook said, "I pass for male or female. . . . When I first came out at seventeen, gender roles were the standard of social interaction. Coming from a southern debutante upbringing, I entered the lesbian scene as a femme.

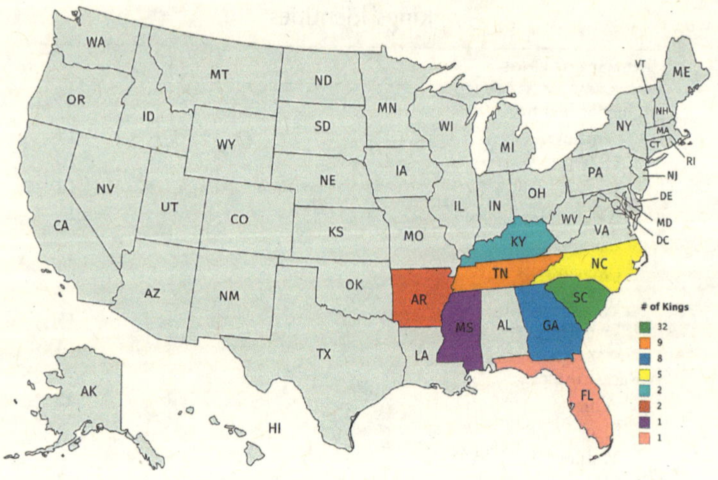

Number of participant kings in the southern United States.

It wasn't until I was twenty did I feel secure enough to embrace my masculinity." Once Shook began to embrace his masculinity, he said, he "emulated hyper masculine thug behavior to fit in" for about five years. Once he began to feel more comfortable, he started to also present his feminine characteristics and behaviors more openly. When I spoke with Shook in 2017, he said that "most people describe [him] as a gay man," and he is okay with that. Shook went on to explain that he is also part of the bondage, discipline, dominance and submission, sadomasochism (BDSM) community and is both a dominant and submissive. He also identified as a lesbian and said that his wife calls him "Big Daddi." He said he hid his attraction to other masculine lesbians until recently, because "as a southern stud you just didn't date other studs."

Another performer, King Axel, a thirty-year-old white queer trans man in South Carolina, described what he means by queer: "I was a lesbian for most of my life, and losing that identity has been difficult, it's like I'm out of my comfort zone, and since I don't have bottom surgery, I find it hard to identify as straight, because honestly I'm probably not something most straight girls would be into . . . so I'm somewhere in between, in this 'queer' area." These examples demonstrate that identities are complex and complicated. A label does not tell us everything about a person, and often labels have different meanings for different people.

A few brief notes that may help when thinking about various combinations of identities of the kings in this study: (1) all of the respondents who identified as heterosexual or straight also identified as trans, meaning they were attracted predominantly to women; (2) the respondents who identified as lesbian also reported attraction mainly to women; (3) if a respondent identified as gay, if they were trans this meant an attraction mainly to men, and if they were cis this meant an attraction mainly to women. These only apply to the kings in this study, not generally. Based on sexual identities, only one respondent, Abs Hart, reported being attracted only to men. Abs said: "I identified as a lesbian for a while before coming out as trans. Once I came out as trans, I allowed myself to realize I was still attracted to men, especially gay men. I'm currently in a gay relationship, and if it ever ended, I would most likely only date gay males." On the contrary, forty-two respondents reported being attracted only or predominantly to women. The remaining seventeen reported attraction to multiple genders, or regardless of gender.

Concerning pronouns, I use he/him/his throughout the book because when the kings are in drag, they prefer masculine pronouns. I use masculine pronouns for consistency, but it is important to note that this book is also concerned with the people who perform drag, not only their drag personas, and these pronouns may or may not match the pronouns the kings use in their everyday lives. For quick reference while reading, you can also refer to the demographic table in appendix A.

♥ CAST OF CHARACTERS ♥

Abs Hart, Arkansas, thirty-five years old, white, transgender male, gay

Drag "helped [me]. Finding out how I was more comfortable. Being that character helped me find things about myself that I was happy about or unhappy about."

Adonis Black, North Carolina, thirty-one years old, multiracial, gender fluid, lesbian

"Drag actually helped me to come out as gender fluid. I feel like I am being me. I used to say my drag persona is my alter ego."

Andrew Star, Florida, thirty-three years old, multiracial, FTM, straight

"Not all that do drag can be placed into a conformed box of gender."

Ayden, South Carolina, forty-four years old, white, female, lesbian

Bastian Sage, Tennessee, twenty-seven years old, white, trans man, straight

Beau Davis, Arkansas, twenty-seven years old, white, trans male and stem,[8] straight

"Drag has helped me transition. It has made it easier to show the true me that I see within myself."

Bo, South Carolina, thirty-eight years old, white, woman, lesbian

Brad Night, South Carolina, forty-three years old, white, male, straight

"I performed because the persona I dressed as was a smooth, confident, strong male, and I wanted to own that identity."

Carson Scott, South Carolina, forty-four years old, Native American, no gender or sexuality label

Chase Down, South Carolina, twenty-nine years old, white, girly or stud, sexuality is open

Chase Sky, Tennessee, twenty-eight years old, white, transgender, straight

Colby King, South Carolina, thirty-three years old, white, female, lesbian

Conner Rush Dupri, South Carolina, twenty-seven years old, white, female, pansexual

Derrick, South Carolina, thirty-five years old, white, female, gay

8. Stem as identity combines the concepts of stud (masculine) and femme (feminine).

Diego Wolf, Georgia, thirty-eight years old, white, transgender man, straight

"I am a huge proponent of using drag as the most safe and effective method to transition into one's [gender] transition to be honest."

D-Luv Saviyon, Tennessee, forty-seven years old, African American, trans man, bisexual

"I do drag because I love to dance and use my creativity to put smiles on people's faces. I have also . . . [used drag] to inspire and advocate. I also do drag as a fun form of escape."

Hayden Fury, Georgia, twenty-eight years old, white, FTM, queer

"I found myself when I started drag, when I noticed I was more comfortable in drag than who I was portraying to be outside of drag."

Hayden Lowe, South Carolina, thirty years old, white, nonconforming/nonbinary, pansexual

"I perform because it allows me to be someone else other than the person I am in everyday life."

Ivan Eatner, South Carolina, twenty-six years old, white, male, straight

"Some do [drag] to express an identity they can't normally express. Some do it as an extension of the identity they already have. I kind of did it as both. As I was starting to come out and pursue a more masculine identity, but it was already there. I also liked doing drag for the performance aspects of it, picking costumes, songs people would like, getting to interact with people."

Jayden Lee Lowe, South Carolina, thirty years old, white, female, lesbian

Jinx Kelly, South Carolina, forty-one years old, white, female, lesbian

JL Evans-Dickerson, North Carolina, thirty-seven years old, African American, female and stem, pansexual

Drag is "a way to escape reality for a moment and be someone else. I am a mother, wife, and friend to so many that at times drag is my only way to leave that for a while."

Johnny Walker, Georgia, twenty-seven years old, Hispanic and white, male, no sexuality label

"It's an art form and freedom of expression. It lets you express a part of yourself that you usually aren't able to show. It let me express some curious feelings that I had about gender."

Jordan Michaels McCord, Georgia, forty-seven years old, white, stud female, lesbian

"I'm still female, living as a female. My drag persona is my outlet to be someone else. I love women and want to stay a woman. Even though my role in a relationship is more of a male's role."

Justin Case, South Carolina, thirty-five years old, white, female, gay

Justin Time, South Carolina, twenty-three years old, white, male, bisexual

"I believe people perform drag because they want to find a way to portray themselves as who they really are. I do it because I love it. I can really be myself."

Kenneth Squires, Kentucky, fifty-three years old, white, female, lesbian

King Axel, South Carolina, thirty years old, white, trans man, queer

"[Drag] helped me deal with a lot of social anxiety (I'm so socially awkward). Drag let me put on this cocky persona and just be someone who didn't give a damn how people saw him or what they thought of him. It was pretty awesome."

Levi Vincent, Tennessee, thirty years old, white, gender neutral, lesbian

"Levi is a more outgoing, flamboyant interpretation of myself. But doing drag has helped me come out of my shell and be more outgoing."

Liquor Down, South Carolina, twenty-eight years old, Hispanic and white, woman, lesbian

LJ Taylor Fury, Georgia, thirty-two years old, white, FTM, queer

"For me, [drag] was always a dream, and me being trans, performing became my home. I felt the most myself when I was in drag. So, it was and still is a creative outlet as well as therapy for dysphoria."

Lucas Storm, South Carolina, thirty years old, white, transvestite, lesbian

Matt Mixer, Tennessee, thirty-one years old, white, male, straight

"[People do drag] to release emotions and create living art when we wear elaborate outfits. To create different characters and escape your life problems for a few hours, to make others smile."

Mike Hunt, Georgia, thirty-four years old, multiracial, male, straight

"I think everybody sees drag as a different escape or therapy. Some use it to get an emotion out, without having to confront it themselves; others just like to dance. Many see it as a different art form. I think at times all of those apply to the reasons behind why I do drag."

Montana, North Carolina, fifty-one years old, white, male, straight

"I did [drag] so people could see me on the outside as the man I knew I was on the inside. I am very quiet and shy. So, [drag] also helped me to hide behind a mask (if you will) to do things I was uncomfortable doing as the female the world saw me as."

Mr. Brightside, South Carolina, twenty-two years old, white, cis female, lesbian

"I wear it proudly, to the point I have a tattoo of me in drag (my narcissistic phase)."

Oliver Clothesoff, South Carolina, thirty-one years old, white and Jewish, female, lesbian

Papi Chulo, Tennessee, twenty-eight years old, Mexican, trans male, pansexual

"[Drag] helped a lot; in many ways I felt more comfortable being Papi Chulo than I did my everyday life, because being in drag and being male up on stage gave me a freedom, made me feel normal. I felt like myself. I still struggle with myself every day, but I love myself, I love that I have to go through this in order to be the man I want to be. [Papi] gave me a lot of life lessons."

Patrick Jacquard, Tennessee, fifty-eight years old, white, female, lesbian

Phil D. Bern, Kentucky, fifty-one years old, African American, male, lesbian

"[Drag] helped because it has helped me walk in my truth."

Prince Dryden, South Carolina, thirty-five years old, white, female, lesbian

Rider Oliver Fox, South Carolina, twenty-five years old, white, mentally male, straight

Rivers Cuomo, South Carolina, thirty-eight years old, white, genderqueer, queer

"I think doing drag helped me access parts of my own masculinity and made masculinity more accessible to me generally."

Romeo, South Carolina, thirty-five years old, multiracial, female, lesbian

Roscoe McCoy, Georgia, forty-five years old, multiracial, gender fluid, omni/pansexual

"For me, [drag] was a means to cast off the proper and professional appearances I maintained and it gave me a means to let loose, express myself artistically, politically, and assume a persona that allows all the things that my vanilla, daytime-self was never allowed to do or say without judgment."

Ryder Cox, South Carolina, thirty-two years old, Native American and white, trans man, straight

"For me, drag started with my dysphoria and eventually grew into me falling in love with the stage and spotlight."

Shawn Lance Hardwood, South Carolina, thirty-one years old, Hispanic, trans FTM, straight

Shawn Stud, Mississippi, thirty-one years old, white, androgynous, bisexual

"I think people do drag for three reasons. First, because it's fun for them. . . . Second, people do drag because it's a way to express a certain part of their identity. . . . Third, some people do drag as work."

Shook ByNature, North Carolina, thirty-five years old, African American, androgynous metrostud, lesbian

"The stage and spotlight give you a high and doing drag can give you an outlet to process what you are going through in real life."

Sir Cameron Sinklair, South Carolina, thirty-six years old, white, man, lesbian

Sir Michael Montgomery, South Carolina, fifty-seven years old, white, female, lesbian

Skyler D. Light, Georgia, thirty-two years old, white, trans male, queer

"I started [performing drag] because I wanted to explore my gender identity, then I found I had a deep love for performance and the drag community."

Soco Dupree, Tennessee, thirty-six years old, white, male, straight

Teddy Michael, North Carolina, thirty-three years old, Black, male, queer

"Drag assisted with my transition evolution on a personal level by giving me more confidence and exposure to more people and things."

Tex, South Carolina, sixty-six years old, white, female, gay or butch

Trey Alize, Tennessee, thirty-five years old, white, gender fluid, lesbian

Warren Payne, South Carolina, thirty-three years old, Pacific Islander and white, female, lesbian

Wes Starr, South Carolina, thirty-four years old, white, non-gender specific, lesbian

Xavier, South Carolina, thirty-eight years old, white, gender neutral, lesbian

Xavier Dupri, South Carolina, thirty-eight years old, white, transgender, straight

Book Overview

Having performed as a drag king in the Southeast myself, I provide a unique perspective on this rarely discussed topic. While the kings I spoke with across the southeastern United States provide the bulk of the material in this book, I also share a behind-the-scenes look

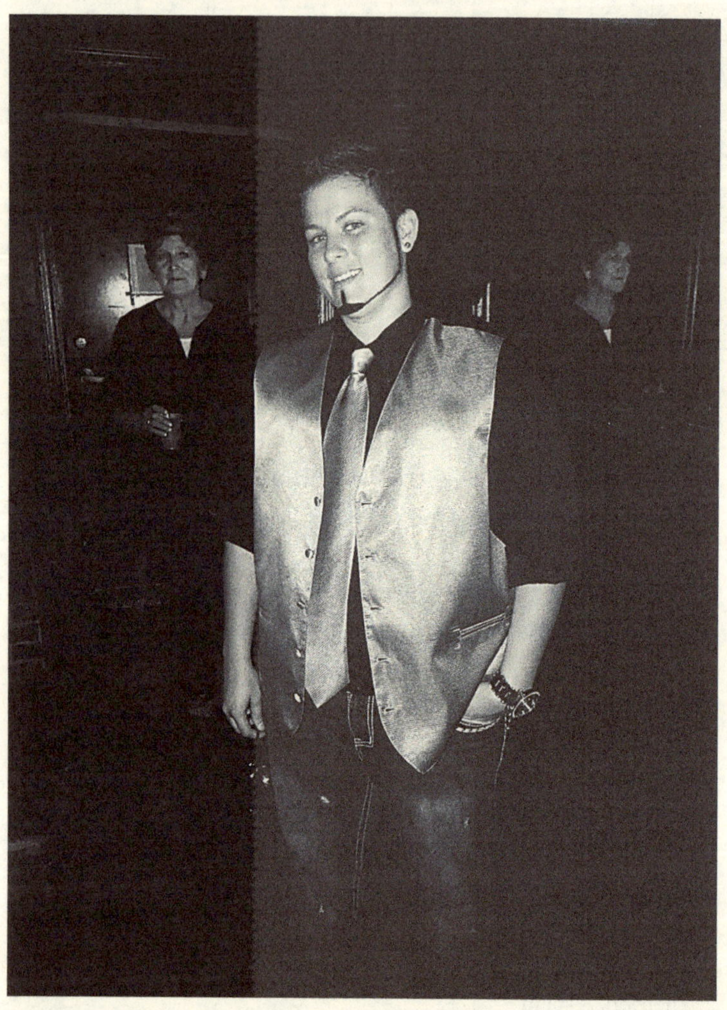

Drag king Hayden Lowe smiles at the camera in a shiny silver tie and vest.

into drag culture from my own perspective. Through the eyes of Macon Love—my drag name and alter ego—I take you on a journey through drag kinging in the Southeast to explore the sociological implications of drag for queer life. The sixty drag kings who talked with me for this book shared their up-close-and-personal views on what it is like to perform drag, but more importantly they talked about what it is like to live outside of the traditional

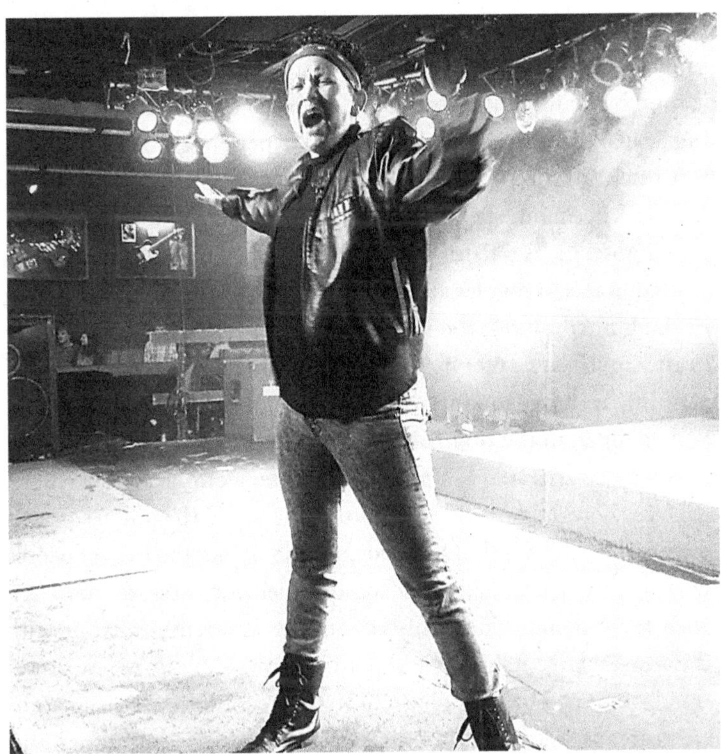

Drag king Macon Loves performs onstage under rainbow-colored lights.

gender and sexual binaries in the South. For more information on the methodology of this study, see appendix B, "My Queer Methodology."

With this book, I am adding to the sparse information on drag kinging by integrating a regional perspective. Some research began to focus on drag kinging as a social phenomenon in the late 1990s, but Troka, Lebesco, and Noble (2002) argued that it was decontextualized and therefore did not provide a complete view of the complexities of drag kinging. In the South, norms emphasizing politeness (Cohen et al. 1999; E. Johnson 2008), an emphasis on family even in nontraditional forms (Weston 1997), a lack of other non-cisgender contexts outside of drag (Rogers 2020), and the lower socioeconomic status and educational levels of the kings and the audiences, combine to form a unique southern dimension to drag kinging that is no less legitimate than other drag king cultures across the country and the world. Through a mixture of storytelling, social scientific analysis, personal experience, and voices from this often-invisible community, you are invited to enter the world of drag kinging in the southern United States.

Chapter 1, "A History of Drag Kinging in the Southeastern United States," provides an overview of the history of drag kinging in the United States, then focuses on the history of drag kinging in the Southeast. Interviews with drag kings who have been performing in the region for over a decade show how drag has grown and changed in the South.

Chapter 2, "Drag Kinging at the Intersections of Identities," explores how drag provides a lens to understand the unique aspects of gender in the South. Drag provides a look into the lives of people who society has turned away because their identities do not align with the cisgender ideals of masculinity and femininity, or with the conservative religious and political values of the region.

Chapter 3, "Drag Kinging as a Resource for Everyday Life," provides an analysis of the importance of drag as a resource for kings to learn about and become comfortable with gender identities and expressions that fall outside of the norms of southern culture. In a region of the country with limited resources for people to learn about gender identity and engage in gender transition, drag provides a community and a place to share knowledge about trans and nonbinary gender identities as well as minority sexual identities. Kings learn about their gender and sexual identities and play with gender through drag in order to figure out what performance fits them best in their everyday lives.

Finally, in chapter 4, "Controversies in the Drag King Community," I examine four controversies within the drag community. First, I look at discussions within the drag king community about what makes a drag king and how one should perform. Then, I examine how identifying as trans has shifted the drag community and how other kings, usually cis lesbian women, react to trans kings.

Next, I explore the tension between drag kings and drag queens within the larger drag community, examining how gender outside of drag often translates into more power or oppression within drag. Finally, I close this chapter with a look at misogyny and homophobia in drag kinging, and how drag can become a celebration of toxic masculinity rather than a critique of it.

1
A History of Drag Kinging in the Southeastern United States

It's drag king night at the queer bar in Columbia, South Carolina. PT's 1109 is primarily a gay men's bar, but since the drag bar and the lesbian bars closed, it is one of the only queer bars left in the city. The bar is hidden away in the back of a tall brick building. You enter through a dark parking lot, and you have to climb up thirty-five steps to reach the door. Locals often refer to the bar as the "trailer in the sky." Once inside, the bar is long, narrow, and dark. There is a wooden bar down the left side stocked with cheap liquor, dancing blocks on the right for scantily clad men, and a small stage directly in front. The atmosphere is dark; everything is black with red accent lights. To brighten the cave-like space, there are strobe lights, a disco ball, a rainbow painted on the wall, and lots of mirrors.

This bar was one of the four queer bars in South Carolina I visited in June 2013 to watch drag kings perform. When I first moved to Columbia in the summer of 2007, there were at least six queer bars in or closely around the city. By the summer of 2010, the one bar that was specifically designated for drag shows closed down. Shortly after, one of the two lesbian bars shut their doors. As of 2019, only two queer bars remained in Columbia: PT's 1109 and the Capital Club, a private gay club that opened in 1980. The Capital

Club's website states that the bar is the longest continuously operating gay bar in the Southeast.

In the forty years since the establishment of the Capital Club, there have been hundreds of queer bars that have opened and (mostly) closed in the Southeast. In fact, there are only two exclusively lesbian bars that remained in the Southeast in 2019, the Lipstick Lounge in Nashville, Tennessee, and My Sister's Room (MSR) in Atlanta, Georgia. This is one reason why three decades after drag king shows gained recognition in queer culture in the United States, the majority of shows still take place in gay male bars (Halberstam 1998). For instance, when I asked Tex where he performed now that a lot of drag bars have disappeared, he said he now relies on a talent booker to find shows when he wants to travel, but that the number of shows available has declined. He said the disappearance of queer bars is especially true for lesbian bars.

D-Luv Saviyon, a forty-seven-year-old African American bisexual trans man, described a similar issue in Nashville, Tennessee. He explained that there were a lot of small queer bars and places to do drag in the early 2000s, but that most them were now closed. D-Luv expounded: "The history of drag in Nashville, I don't really know how it started, but the history of drag in Nashville actually was pretty strong because when I came out, there were a lot of small bars, and then Connections was the main big bar. You had Trax, you had Connections, and then some of the other clubs came about. . . . There was . . . a place called Mama's Kitchen, so we would go there. There was a place called the 19th Hole, so it was just little places around."

D-Luv explained that drag queens were well known in Nashville at that time: "I know as far as the history of drag, I mean like the legend here is that . . . Connections had the biggest shows. They had—just like queens that were people who you would think that they were just regular women on stage. I know that [Nashville] was a big [drag] pageant town for a long time too, in the '90s. . . . It was just a whole bunch of people that were legends then." Even today, D-Luv said, the quick turnover of queer bars in the Nashville area continues: "Connections is still the main club. We have a couple now . . . like Pecker's—they have drag. Trax is still around. Well, Connections is gone, but Play is there. Trax still has a drag show, mostly on Sundays. Now, it's just kind of a pop-up show here and there, sometimes that happens. There's another place called Fusion, that's in Clarksville. I perform there on occasion and they have a twice a month drag show which features kings. . . . There used to be a couple of other clubs in the last couple years, but they've closed."

Understanding the history of queer bars in the region is a complicated task. Many people in the Southeast lived their entire lives in towns with queer bars but never knew they existed. For instance, in Rock Hill, South Carolina, the queer bar is down a dirt road in a mobile home park. In Cayce, South Carolina, one of the lesbian bars was in a quiet residential area in a windowless warehouse with no signage. Therefore, to learn about the history of queer bars and drag in the region, you have to speak to the locals and piece together a complicated history of struggle and turnover.

One city in the Southeast that has a little more of a record of a queer scene is Atlanta, Georgia. Lena Lust, a famous drag queen from Atlanta, explained to *Atlanta Magazine* (Reeves 2010) that "2000 was the beginning of the start of the fall, when the big change happened with the big bars closing—the closing of Backstreet and a few other places. It just took it down from the straight bars down to the gay bars, to eventually where we are now with the small venues. It's just very hard now. I think if we can just continue to fight, we can make it. We've got people out there fighting for us. If the gay community pulled together and did their part, we can get back to maybe halfway where we were before, but not all the way." The "beginning of the start of the fall" of the gay bars and clubs in the Southeast, according to Lena Lust, occurred simultaneously with the beginning of drag kinging in the region. Just as drag kinging started to take off, the bars and clubs began to close.

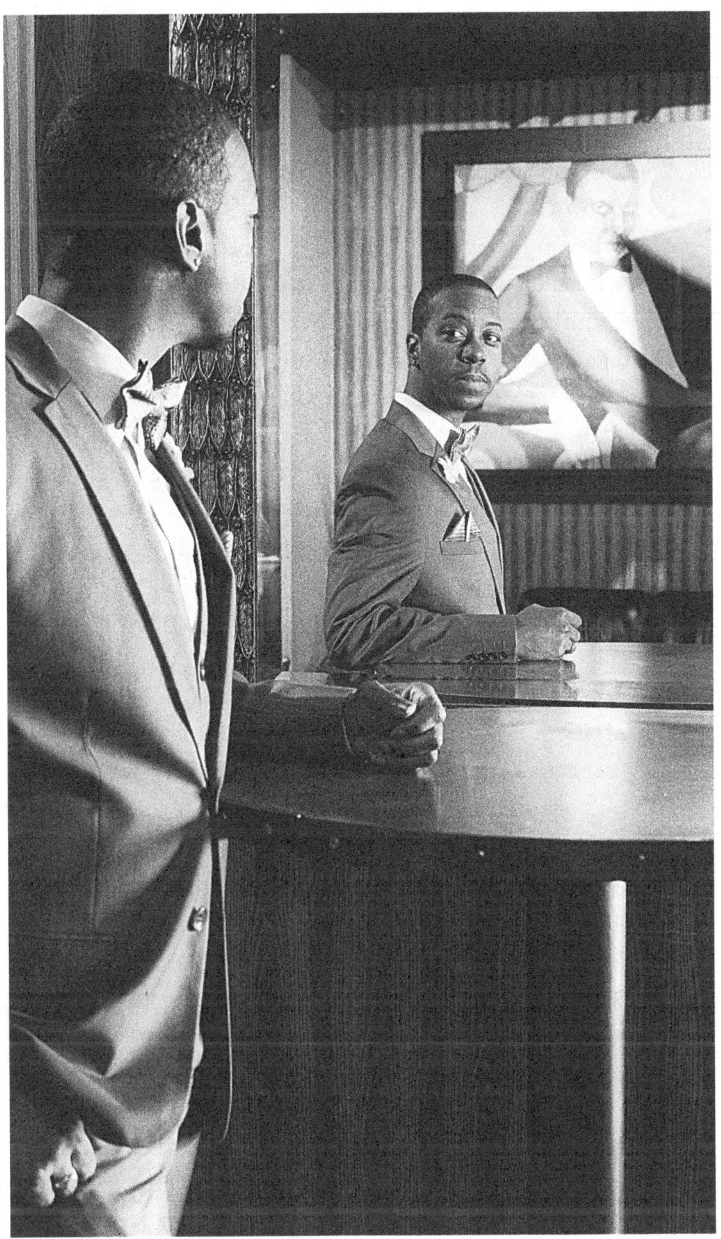

Drag king D-Luv Saviyon wears a blue suit and looks at self in mirror.

Patrick Jacquard explained why he thought there had been a major decline in queer bars in the Southeast and in the country more generally during the 2000s:

> I believe they closed, especially the actual gay bars themselves, because we've seen more progressive people. What's happened over the years, we were all, back in my day, back in the '70s and '80s, we could only go to gay bars. If we didn't feel comfortable being with our partner at a restaurant or sports bar or anything like that, because this thing is like, this is very awkward. It wasn't accepted. As things progress and we used to have other places where we can go and be ourselves, I think that people just didn't feel like they had to go to the gay bar all the time. I think it's bad that they don't support them because when they're gone, people always say, "Well, you know, we should have supported it." Well, you didn't and now you don't have it. That's probably the biggest reason, I think, is because people just have so many other places they can go. Now you're having shows in sports bars, having drag brunches in other places that are not gay bars. That's the gist of it, local reasons I think that they're closing. They just can't keep that business. When you're the only place to go, that's one thing. When you're in a city where there's other venues that you can go and do drag in with your partner, your wife, your husband, then you don't have to feel like you have to just support that one, even though they should, but they don't.

So, while progressive change is good, in Patrick's opinion, it has killed the queer bar. Patrick places most of the blame on queer people for not supporting other queer people and places. Whatever or whomever is to blame, the decline of the queer bar at the beginning of modern drag kinging in the South led to a relatively brief moment in the spotlight for most kings in the area. Of course, drag kinging, or its close relative male impersonation, did not begin in the early 2000s; that is just when it gained some notice in the southeastern United States.

History of Drag Kinging

The first recorded male impersonator in the United States was Annie Hindle, who began to perform in variety shows in 1868 after arriving from England (Rodger 2018). In fact, the term "male impersonator" did not become widely used until 1870, when a second male impersonator, Ella Wesner, created competition for Hindle's act. Rodger (2018, 29) describes Hindle's performances this way: "She dressed in realistic male costume and delivered songs in a low alto voice, interrupting the song text with pun-filled monologues, jokes, and topical asides to further develop the character she portrayed." As precursors to modern-day drag kings, Hindle and Wesner opened the door for women to perform as men in the United States, since both men and women vastly enjoyed their shows and made them famous across the variety circuits of their time. Performing as men, male impersonators also opened the door to comedy for women (Rodger 2018). While Rodger (2018, 11) argues that male impersonators "trespassed on the traditionally male ground of comedy," I would add that, even more importantly, they trespassed on the traditionally male ground of masculinities.

There were limits, however, to the degree that early male impersonators could trespass on masculinities. Most early male impersonators presented themselves as immature boys, not "real" men (Halberstam 1998). While female impersonators and drag queens have always been allowed to perform representations of adult femininities, male impersonators were not encouraged to present "the plausible representation of mannishness" (Halberstam 1998, 233). This meant that "mature masculinity once again remains an authentic property of male bodies while all other gender roles are available for interpretation" (Halberstam 1998, 233).

The performances of early male impersonators in the United States were also not strictly tied to the performer's own gender or sexual identities. While there is evidence that some of the male impersonators of the late nineteenth and early twentieth centuries may have been sexually attracted to women, there is also evidence that they were attracted to men (Rodger 2018). Modern-day definitions of gender and sexuality do not easily translate to these early predecessors of drag. Therefore, while some early male impersonators in the United States may have been seen as more masculine, or as attracted to women, male impersonation was not always tied to gender and sexual identities.

Although male impersonators were the forerunners of drag kings, it is important to differentiate the two types of performances. Male impersonators received wide acclaim on the variety show circuit from the emergence of Annie Hindle in 1868 through the 1920s. However, in 1933 the Hollywood Motion Picture Production Code was passed, which "banned all performances of so-called sexual perversion," and this led to the disappearance of male impersonation from variety shows (Halberstam 1998, 234). It would take another sixty years for drag kings to gain recognition within queer culture. When drag kings began to emerge within the queer bar scene in the early 1990s, they also differed from male impersonators in that drag kings often parodied masculinities and attempted to show them as performances, rather than to present "a plausible performance of maleness" like those of male impersonators (Halberstam 1998, 232).

Traditionally, drag was defined as an incongruence between a performer's biological sex and the gender they were performing on stage (Halberstam 1998; Newton 1979). Therefore, drag kings were assumed to be female-bodied and woman identified outside of their performances. As Jack Halberstam (1998, 236) argues, "In a drag performance . . . incongruence becomes the site of gender creativity." Likewise, as late as 2007, Eve Shapiro continued to define drag kings as female-bodied people who performed masculinities as an act. Due to this history, most audience members today continue to assume an incongruence between the gender performance and the performer's biological sex. Hence, drag kings are largely imagined to be female-bodied and to identify as women, and usually lesbian women, outside of their drag performances. Although these assumptions have never been completely accurate, they were based on some reality at the beginning of the drag king scene in the United States in the 1990s.

In the 1990s, drag king culture, which Halberstam (1997, 106) describes as "necessarily multiple," became "something of a subcultural phenomenon" in the United States (Halberstam 1998, 232). Drag kinging began largely within lesbian subcultures and provided an outlet for lesbian women to perform masculinities (Drysdale 2019; Halberstam 1997, 1998). By the 1990s, queer bars in major cities around the world had begun to feature kings. However, it is difficult to trace the precise beginnings of the term "drag king," largely because of the invisibility of female masculinities and lesbian subcultures, which led to local communities developing in relative isolation from one another, and thereby in disparate ways. Because "forms of erasure continue to have a defining impact on lesbian life in the twenty-first century" (Drysdale 2019, 5), it is vital to trace the history of drag kings in various regions of the world. Scholars must ensure that these scenes and experiences are captured in the history of our regions and various communities, especially in queer history. This is also likely why a number of drag kings from various regions claim to have started the usage of the term and to have been the first king to perform in the United States. As Kerryn Drysdale (2019, 25) explains, due to the variable starts of drag kinging around the world, "it is not possible to definitively track the rising popularity of drag king culture from a single event, performer, or place."

Drag kings, at least in the South, are no longer primarily female-bodied or woman identified. Now more than ever, drag performers present a wide range of gender and sexual identities and expressions, both in drag and outside of drag. Furthermore, the lines between male impersonation and drag kinging have been largely blurred, which I will discuss in more detail in a moment. Examining drag kings in Australia, Drysdale (2019, 23) writes that today, "who counts as a drag king is diverse across different times and locales, . . . his performances are practiced and recognized unevenly, and the contexts with which he is associated [shift] depending on his audiences."

Despite the uncertainty around the first use of "drag king," most scholars agree that the act of drag kinging did not reach critical mass in the United States, and likely around the world, until the 1990s due to the combination of the marginalization of lesbians and the conflation of white males with masculinity (Halberstam 1998; Shapiro 2007). Nevertheless, as Roscoe McCoy explained in an interview, "Male drag has not been something that just popped up after *RuPaul's Drag Race* and stuff started coming out. If you go back . . . to the early days, speakeasies and Harlem and other stuff like that, there were drag kings, but they worked hard. . . . History has suppressed so much of that, even queer history." Roscoe is correct that drag kinging is not new, and that queer history has been neglected in many ways, leaving large gaps in our understanding of drag and other forms of queer performance.

Drag kinging's distinctive history from drag queening has likewise produced distinctive ideas about gender performativity. Drag queening has a longer traceable history than the performance of drag kinging. The term "drag queen" is thought to have originated in the 1930s as part of gay men's bar culture (Rupp and Taylor 2003). Like the history of drag kings, however, the history of queer drag queens is also linked to theatrical cross-dressing in the late nineteenth century (Senelick 2000). Nevertheless, the distinction between drag queens and drag kings is important because femininity has always been presented as an act and a costume, while "masculinity manifests as realism or as body" (Halberstam 1998, 258).

Given the divergent origins and goals of drag kings and queens, it is important to examine how each type of performance presents unique challenges to the binary gender system in society (Willox 2002). While drag queens and kings are both theatrical, this theatricality occurs in "opposite directions," as drag kinging requires "performing nonperformativity" (Halberstam 1998, 259). Femininities in drag are viewed as funny and entertaining, while creating performative and entertaining masculinities is still a feat many kings struggle to accomplish. Some of the kings in this study articulated this opposition of performativity between femininities and masculinities. For instance, Justin Case said, "Drag queens can have a large liberty with how fabulous they can make themselves with wigs and sequined dresses and makeup and heels and all sorts of things that drag queens can kind of go out and do, whereas drag kings, especially the younger ones, would settle for like not very elaborate costumes. They felt like being a drag king meant just dressing like a man, just like [an] everyday man at the mall. It's just not entertaining."

Drag kings continue to struggle to gain the same recognition as drag queens, and drag kings continue to be "relegated to a subcultural or underground phenomenon in comparison to the more visible drag queen form" (Drysdale 2019, 26). As Mac Huffington, a promoter of drag kings in Nashville, Tennessee, explains, "The popularity of drag kings / male illusionists has risen greatly, but the struggle is still to get them equal bookings and pay comparable to the drag queens" (quoted in Grady 2019). It seems that in drag culture, power and prestige are linked to the assumed biological sex and gender identity underneath the performance, not the gender being performed. Drag queens, who are assumed to be male-bodied and to identify as men outside of drag, continue to earn more attention, pay, and tips, and hold a higher level of prestige within queer culture than drag kings.

Roscoe McCoy provided an example of when he tried to join the drag scene in Augusta, Georgia: "The queens run the scene, so if you don't get in with queens, you don't get stage time. You don't get a shot. . . . If you didn't kiss ass for certain queens, you weren't in the clique. You couldn't get into a bar, you couldn't get booked . . . if you're not approved by them, if you're not their darling, you don't get in on a stage." Roscoe went on to say, "It's almost kind of like a role reversal. We deal with it, the irony of it; in everyday culture, we deal with misogyny and female presentation for a lot of us in our workplace and culturally and everything like that. We get an avenue to express masculinity, but that avenue was run by drag queens who kind of throw that back. Now, we're kind of role reversing, so the male presenting entertainers don't have a place."

Overall, drag kings and drag king culture have not reached the level of pop culture familiarity, popularity, and visibility that drag queens and drag queen culture have gained. Drag queens, most of

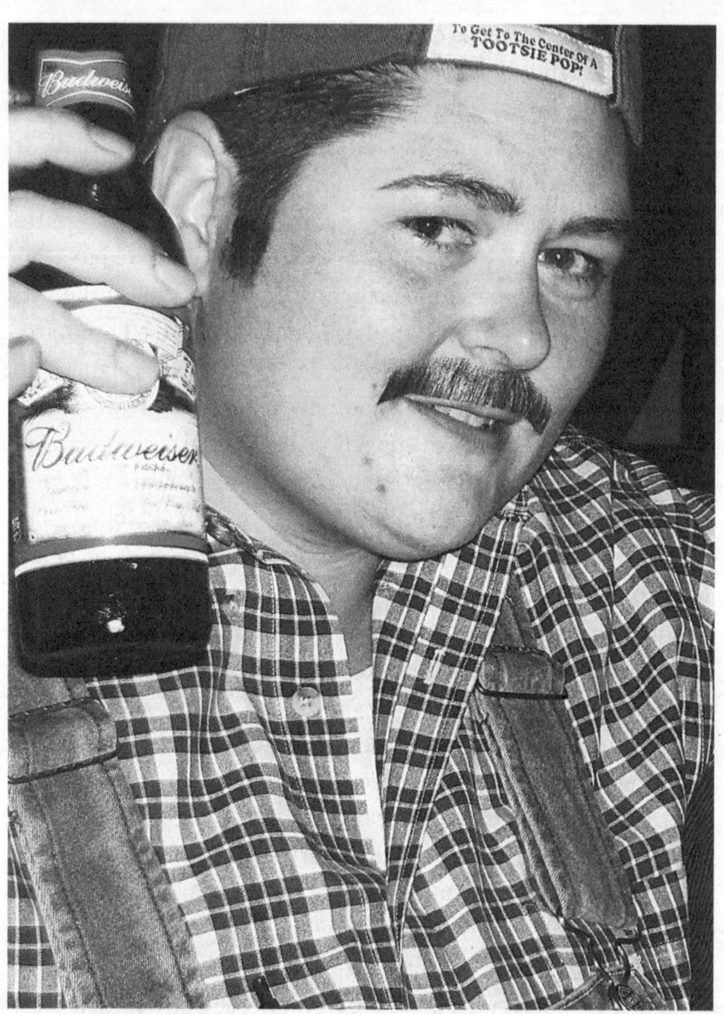

Drag king Roscoe McCoy raises a beer to the camera.

whom are male-bodied and present as cis men outside of drag, continue to have more power and resources than drag kings. This is largely related to gender inequality in work and pay, as well as unequal wealth between men and women. For instance, Carpenter and Eppink (2017) found that between 2013 and 2015, the average annual earnings for heterosexual men were $57,032, for gay men $59,618, for heterosexual women $39,902, and for lesbian women

$47,026. So, even when taking into account possible minority sexual identities, gay men are still making significantly more than both heterosexual women and lesbian women ($19,716 and $12,592 annually, respectively). Income and wealth inequality mean that drag queens and gay men generally have more money and resources to put into their drag performances and to own and frequent bars where drag shows occur, and are likely to have more leisure time to prepare for shows and frequent shows than drag kings and lesbian women. Relatedly, cis gay men, like RuPaul, are more likely to get TV deals than trans men or lesbian women. Most people in the United States continue to view femininities as more of a performance, and thereby as more entertaining, than masculinities. The outrageousness of femininities performed in drag typically leads to more audience members and more tips for queens than kings. Finally, the continued stigma around trans people performing drag, which I discuss in more detail in chapter 4, seems to be a bigger issue for kings in the South than for queens. While some drag queens are trans, the growing popularity of drag kinging for trans men has meant that some people do not take kinging as seriously as queening.

Relatedly, there remains an ongoing debate regarding whether camp is available for "lesbian appropriation," or in drag kinging more broadly (Halberstam 1998). Camp, according to Susan Sontag (1964; quote from Smith 2019), is "an embrace of all things exaggerated, artificial, and over-the-top." The goal of camp is to be entertaining and amusing by performing in a way that is outrageous, overdone, or inappropriate. In the popular imagination, camp is predominantly associated with drag and ballroom culture. Erika Smith (2019) explains, "It's impossible to discuss camp without looking at the influence of queer folks, particularly queer and trans people of color. . . . [But importantly,] while some types of queer fashion and culture, like drag, are camp—and camp can be real art—not everything queer is camp." Camp is about parody and demonstrating the ridiculousness of normative expectations. Because camp is about exaggerated performance, Halberstam (1998, 237–238) argues, "camp is always about femininity."

For illustration, the drag king shows I attended in the South were often hosted by a drag queen to add more humor and entertainment. The queens almost always discussed things that would be viewed as inappropriate to most people, especially in the South. The queens I have seen host shows love to talk mainly about sex and their genitalia. In the summer of 2013, one of the king shows I attended was cohosted by a drag queen, Anya. Anya was a very attractive Black drag queen who was well known in Columbia, South Carolina. After she was introduced, she appeared on stage in a black bodysuit and tall boots to perform Lil' Kim's song "How Many Licks." Some of the lyrics to the song are "I've been a lot of places, seen a lot of faces, Ah, hell I even fucked with different races, A white dude—his name was John, He had a Queen Bee Rules tattoo on his arm." Following this performance, Anya interacted with the audience, asking audience members to pull something out "from way down in my vajayjay" and calling on audience members with birthdays to come up front to "have their cherries popped." Anya then took shots with those who came up to celebrate birthdays, explaining that "shots make my vagina wet." While her cohost, Ayden, also performed camp in some ways, Anya was definitely viewed as being the headline and most hilarious.

Nevertheless, there has been a dramatic shift in drag king culture over the last thirty years, and drag kings are finally reaching a moment when the outrageousness of masculinities can be performed and accepted, at least within drag and queer cultures. Drag kings' performances go beyond the limited "strategies to render masculinity visible and theatrical" that Halberstam (1998, 238) was able to envision in the 1990s. Even in the conservative region of the southeastern United States, drag kinging can be, and often is, camp. For instance, Oliver Clothesoff, a thirty-one-year-old white Jewish lesbian woman who performs in South Carolina, describes his performances as camp. Oliver said, "I feel like I'm on the campier side. I do a lot of Aaron Carter and parodies and everything. If it's a top forty song, it's gonna have a weird twist to it, like, it's gonna have a crazy costume or it's gonna be weird. I like that there is no one here like me, so I can just let my freak flag fly, and you know no one cares and that's what I really like is just getting to do the strange stuff."

In June 2013, I saw Oliver Clothesoff perform at PT's 1109 in Columbia, South Carolina. He was the only king that night who used costumes rather than street clothes. He danced and was far more dramatic than the other kings, which really seemed to pay off when it came to tips from the audience. Oliver performed a Harry Potter parody to the Far East Movement song "Like a G6," titled "Like It's Quidditch." He dressed in a Harry Potter costume and was carrying a stick for his wand around the bar. Next, he performed a Macklemore and Ryan Lewis hip-hop song, "Thrift Shop." He was dressed like he just stepped out of a thrift store dressing room. At the end of the song, Oliver pulled his wig off and let his long brown hair down, breaking the illusion of masculinity.

Drag Kinging in the South

Drag kings started performing in the South in the 1990s, as in other areas of the country, but most people, even queer people, did not know about drag kinging in this region until the early 2000s. While there are a number of similarities between drag kings in the South and other regions of the country and the world, regional variations in drag kinging are important. Because female masculinities (and trans and nonbinary masculinities) developed in relative isolation to one another, in hidden subcultures around the United States and around the world, drag kinging, and queer culture more generally, looks different based on region and context (Ayoup and Podmore 2002; Halberstam 1998; E. Johnson 2008; Piontek 2002). This is why early attempts to understand drag kinging based only on kings from major metropolitan areas cannot provide an overarching framework for understanding this type of performance (Piontek 2002). For instance, Halberstam's (1999) claim that drag kinging only lives in "cities that never sleep" is limited at best (Piontek 2002). As I find in this study of Southern drag kings, Piontek (2002) also found that in smaller cities and communities in the Midwest there are thriving drag king scenes. Hence, as Drysdale

(2019, 29) suggests, "Rather than attempting to secure a universal definition that covers all drag king practices and their various historical antecedents, it is more useful to focus on some of its vagaries as they play out in local, rather than global, contexts."

Labeling queer culture as urban is not limited to drag but is applied to queer culture more broadly (Howard 1999; E. Johnson 2008). The assumption that queer cultures only flourish in large urban areas on the East and West coasts of the United States obscures the significant and ongoing presence of queer Southerners (E. Johnson 2008; Stone 2018). This metronormative bias also limits the consideration of how rural life, religion, and race intersect with various queer cultures. One of my goals for this book is to expand our understanding of drag and queer life outside of the big cities and into a region from which queer people are generally expected to flee (Kazyak 2012). To do this, I start by providing the history of drag kinging in the Southeast according to the kings themselves.

Patrick Jacquard was the second oldest drag king in this study, and one of two who claims to have been the first, or at least among the first, drag kings in the country. Although he began performing as a king decades before, Patrick Jacquard explained, "I think the '90s was basically when we saw more [kings] coming out." While a couple of kings, including Patrick, performed as early as the late 1960s and 1970s, the majority of Southern kings I interviewed agreed that drag kinging did not really take off in the South until the early 2000s.

While all of the drag kings discussed in this book explained how they got their start doing drag, I conducted follow-up interviews with six drag kings in the Southeast who had been performing drag in the region for at least ten years and were at least thirty years old. These interviews took place in December 2018 and January 2019. The kings were from South Carolina (1), Mississippi (1), Tennessee (2), and Georgia (2), and they helped me piece together much of the Southern history of drag kinging in the United States. Here I discuss this specific history of drag kinging in the South according to the kings I spoke with between 2013 and 2019, with a focus on the six kings who have been performing in the area for over a decade.

Tex claimed to be the first drag king to perform in South Carolina, if not the first in the entire country. He began performing in 1969 at the Fortress Club in Columbia. Ten years later, Patrick Jacquard performed publicly as a drag king for the first time at a little club called the DePriest Lounge in Tupelo, Mississippi. Patrick said he always knew he wanted to be a drag king, even before he knew what that meant. He explained, "For me, it was a pretty early age . . . like, thirteen or fourteen, because I've always been a tomboy, and . . . I remember back then just playing some of the songs like the Grass Roots, and different artists, especially the male artists. I would find myself lip-synching to them, and acting out, and dancing. I think that I just really enjoyed doing that, but I didn't have a clue, at that point in time, that there were even things for drag kings. As a matter of fact, there weren't any drag kings at all." Patrick went on: "I don't think there were ever any [drag kings]. Matter of fact, I might have been one of the first couple that I knew of in the United States."

When Patrick started performing in Tupelo in 1979, he said it was at "a Black club, predominantly a Black club, and [the owner] didn't have enough business, so he let the gay people come in there." He said that in 1979 in a little club in Tupelo, "the crowds just went crazy, because they'd seen queens, but they never saw a [king] transformation, and . . . I've always made, I think, a really good transformation. For me, it's like, you have to do it, and do it right, or don't do it at all, and that's what I did." After performing in Tupelo, Patrick moved to Atlanta in 1979, where he and "one other girl" started performing at Sweet Gum Head, an Atlanta gay bar that has been described as "the Las Vegas show club of the South" (Reeves 2010). He said, "Oh my gosh, so many legends, their own cast, which are now really legends to us." He started performing at Sweet Gum Head every Wednesday night on their open night.

After returning to Mississippi from Atlanta, Patrick opened his own show bar, O'Hara's, in Shannon, Mississippi, in 1994. Soon after, Patrick opened another club called Casablanca in Memphis,

Tennessee, and briefly an outpost of O'Hara's in Columbus, Mississippi. Patrick ran the original O'Hara's for four years, in a small, rural town in Mississippi about ten miles from Tupelo where he first performed. In 1998, Patrick sold the bar. The new owners changed the name to Rumors, and it remained open in the town until 2010. In fact, the bar was the subject of the 2006 documentary *Small Town Gay Bar.* Patrick said, "You've got to have that stage, you got to give the entertainers a place to be themselves to perform. . . . My stage is always open." Patrick tried to reopen O'Hara's in Shannon in 2013, but was denied a license by the town. Patrick filed a federal lawsuit against the town for violating his civil rights to free speech and equal protection (Ward 2013). In an article on the lawsuit, Patrick is quoted saying, "If I'd been a straight redneck from Shannon, nobody would have cared" (Ward 2013). The case was privately settled in 2014, and Patrick was not allowed to reopen O'Hara's in Shannon. Today, Patrick runs O'Hara's Entertainment, where he is a drag promoter and schedules shows across Mississippi and the Southeast. One of Patrick's biggest shows now is in Starkville, Mississippi, home of Mississippi State University, where I completed my PhD and met Patrick. I performed in a couple of his first shows in Starkville in 2014 and 2015. In addition to Starkville, Patrick takes drag kings and queens to Bowling Green, Kentucky; Oxford, Mississippi; Birmingham, Alabama; Nashville, Tennessee; and elsewhere.

Patrick said he continues to work as a promoter because he loves the work, and if he does not take drag shows to small towns in the region, most people will not be able to experience them. He explained:

> It takes a promoter to come into these towns, because these kids have nothing, especially in the college towns where they have to drive. Bowling Green has to drive to Nashville, which is forty-five minutes to an hour. If you drink and go out, then you're driving back. The whole point is they do it, but [they shouldn't be] drinking and driving. They enjoy when the shows are local and when they're good. I like to bring in headliners

that are actually known queens, so they get a little of both. That's what the show's about. You get the great drag queens with the costuming and then you give everybody else a chance to perform. . . . We've got the beginners, we've got the middle guys, and then we've got the professionals. Everybody gets something from it.

Patrick said that he is the only promoter he knows of doing these traveling drag shows. He said he targets college towns because "the kids that are in the college seem to be more interested. It gives them a place. Not only as a college town that doesn't have a bar, it gives the kids a place to go that are coming out. It's an outlet for them. . . . Some of them have never seen a drag show."

Tex returned to South Carolina in 2003, after years of traveling the world as a professional wrestler. Tex said, "Whenever I made home base out in Columbia, South Carolina, I started going to one club and started talking to some of the queens that were coming up from Florida, and they started bringing me up on stage to perform with them. At that time, some of them would help me with what they wanted me to look like when we'd go on stage for their song." Before that, he had been performing in other countries, such as Singapore, New Zealand, and Australia. However, Tex explained, "I actually did not notice [kings] were as big in the States until 2003. . . . I'd bugged the Gay Pride in South Carolina since 2000, 'Why don't you give the women a shot? It's not just the boys that want to be girls, there's some girls out there that do a heck of a job, because I've seen them overseas.' They . . . said, 'You're seeing them overseas; they're not here.' I said, 'They're out there; they're just not coming out, because they don't think there is a place for them.'" After three years of persistence, Tex persuaded the director of South Carolina Pride to give kings a shot. In 2003, South Carolina Pride held the first *Mr.* and Mrs. Gay Pride Pageant. That year only Tex and one other king competed for the title, but the following year there were nine local pageants in the state to send representatives to Mr. and Mrs. Gay Pride. That same year, Tex recruited four performers for the first drag king show in the state and formed a drag king troupe—a group of drag kings and/or queens who perform together on a regular basis—Tex and the Capital City Kings, which performed regularly at PT's Cabaret, a gay bar in Columbia. According to Tex, "My thinking in the Southeast is that once I made King of South Carolina, everybody came out of the woodwork. Whenever they saw me getting recognized, then all the other states in the Southeast" started having drag kings compete.

That same year is when Diego Wolf was first introduced to drag kinging and began performing in Athens, Georgia. Diego, now a thirty-eight-year-old white transgender man, moved to Athens for graduate school when he was twenty-one and met a couple of local kings through one of his classes. He was introduced to some other "young trans guys" who were working on starting up a drag king troupe. Diego was invited to perform at "an open-mic night for drag" at the local gay bar and ended up winning the competition. After he won the competition, the other guys invited Diego to join the troupe, and they formed the first drag king troupe in Athens, the Classic City Kings. Before they started the Classic City Kings, a few kings performed in Athens with the local queens, but according to Diego, "the prominence of drag kings did not start until the early 2000s." Diego said he has been performing drag ever since. Unfortunately, though, Diego said that he performed at "the only gay bar in the history of Athens"—Boneshakers—and it closed down in 2005, less than two years after he started performing drag. Diego says there are now two Athens bars that allow kings to perform, Go Bar and Wayward, but still, fifteen years later no one has opened another queer bar in the city.

While drag kinging thrived in Columbia, South Carolina, for a while after Tex got it started up in 2003, he said it has definitely declined in popularity now. When I lived in Columbia, I was lucky to witness this brief period when drag kinging was thriving in the area, from 2007 to 2011. My first performance as a drag king was at PT's Cabaret, the major hub for drag kings in Columbia. But when PT's Cabaret closed in 2010, there was no equivalent to replace it. While other bars featured drag kings in the city, many have closed or host kings only once a week. Tex said, "We live in Columbia; it's fallen down. [Drag kings] don't have anybody to direct them, but the queens try to help them, but the queens don't know how to help the girls to be boys." Tex explained that the only two places left for drag kings to perform in Columbia are PT's 1109 and the new bar, Vice, which opened in the space occupied by the closed down bar L-Word. Tex summarized: "Drag kings, they didn't start hitting the air until 2003. . . . For the East Coast [now], it's gone like a dying breed again. There's not that many that I can find. . . . The East Coast just ain't staying up with the rest of the country, or I should say, South Carolina." Tex went on to discuss his frustration with the South Carolina drag king scene: "In Columbia it's just like, they can come out when they need a girlfriend. Once they get a girlfriend, it's like, 'Well, I don't perform anymore.' . . . Some of the people, they'd get in relationships, they can't perform, because they don't want their girlfriends flirting with another girl to get a tip. In North Carolina, most of the people, they've been in some long-term relationships, so they know that they don't have to worry about their partners."

Chattanooga, Tennessee, was where Roscoe McCoy was first introduced to drag. He said that he learned about drag in the early 1990s from queens at a club called Alan Gold's: "It was the first drag show I'd ever saw live and in person. I was like nineteen, twenty years old at the time." Roscoe explained, "There weren't a lot of drag kings to learn a lot of male illusion from. I had made friends with a lot of the drag queens at Backstreet [a gay club in Atlanta] in the early '90s." The third floor of Backstreet was turned into Charlie Brown's Cabaret in 1991, "featuring the best in Atlanta's drag scene" (Bagby 2016). Roscoe said, "There were never any drag kings at Charlie Brown's that I ever saw. Not because it never happened, but none that I ever saw. . . . Even back then, if you wanted to be a drag queen, and be taken seriously, you had to work to get into it. You had to prove that you were dedicated, that it wasn't just like some little phase that you were going through or anything like that, and that you dedicated time to putting together performance pieces and costume-making and the real over the top glitz and glam of it." This is where Roscoe learned the ins and outs of drag, and why he has some strong opinions on drag kings today who do not put in the amount of effort he believes is required for performance. Backstreet was open twenty-four hours a day, and "was the last of the big bars." It closed down in 2004 (Reeves 2010).

Roscoe said that his "first exposure" to drag kings was in Atlanta around "2003, maybe going into 2004" at the Moxy show. "I guess, logically, it should've made sense that if you can have female, you can also have male gender illusion. It had never really clicked with me, until I saw cabaret for the first time, and I'm like, 'Now, that looks like that was so much fun, and why didn't you think about this?'" He did not think of it because he "had never seen anybody do male illusion any earlier than the end of the early 2000s and up." He said, "Ten whole years here in the 90s that I was going to gay bars around the South, and I never saw anybody do male drag until then. If it was there . . . it was rare, rare enough that I didn't see it."

In Nashville, Tennessee, D-Luv Saviyon said, "I think the year that I saw the first king, it had to be probably around, oh God, '99." In 2000, D-Luv was "approached by a really well-known drag king troupe . . . to do some choreography for them and teach them dances. They were called Anonymous Man." He helped them with choreography and danced backup for a couple of them and got "hooked" on drag. After that, in 2001, he and another king started a group called Dos Playbois, and he performed as a king for the first time. D-Luv explained, "That's how it started. A little club named Amnesia, which is no longer here either."

Trey Alize, a thirty-five-year old white gender fluid lesbian in Nashville, Tennessee, was the last to be introduced to drag out of the six kings I interviewed in more depth about the history of drag kinging in the Southeast. After he graduated from college in 2007, he was going to a bar in Nashville called the Cabaret, which he described as "pretty much the lesbian bar back in the day." One night, he witnessed his "first ever drag show" and made an offhand comment to a friend that he could do that. That friend immediately signed him up for the next show and told him to "put his

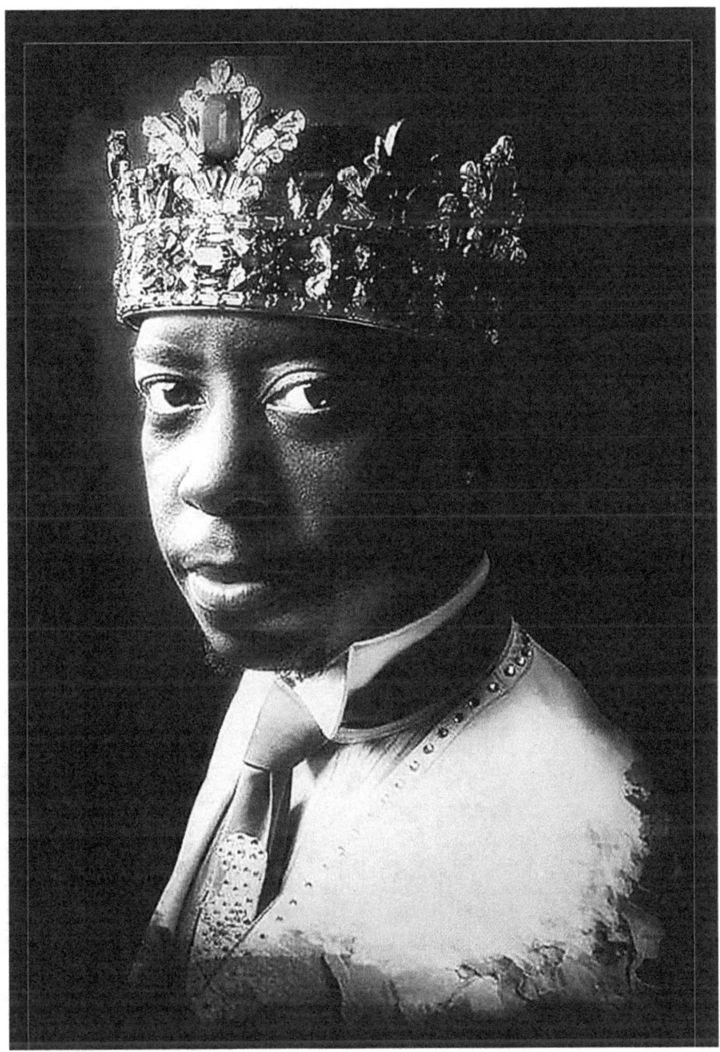

Drag king D-Luv Saviyon poses in his recently won crown.

money where his mouth is." Although the Cabaret closed only about a year later, Trey has been performing drag in Nashville ever since that first show in 2007. He said, "As far as drag kings in our community, it's a very young community. . . . Play Dance Bar and the Cabaret were our two bars that we mostly performed at." In

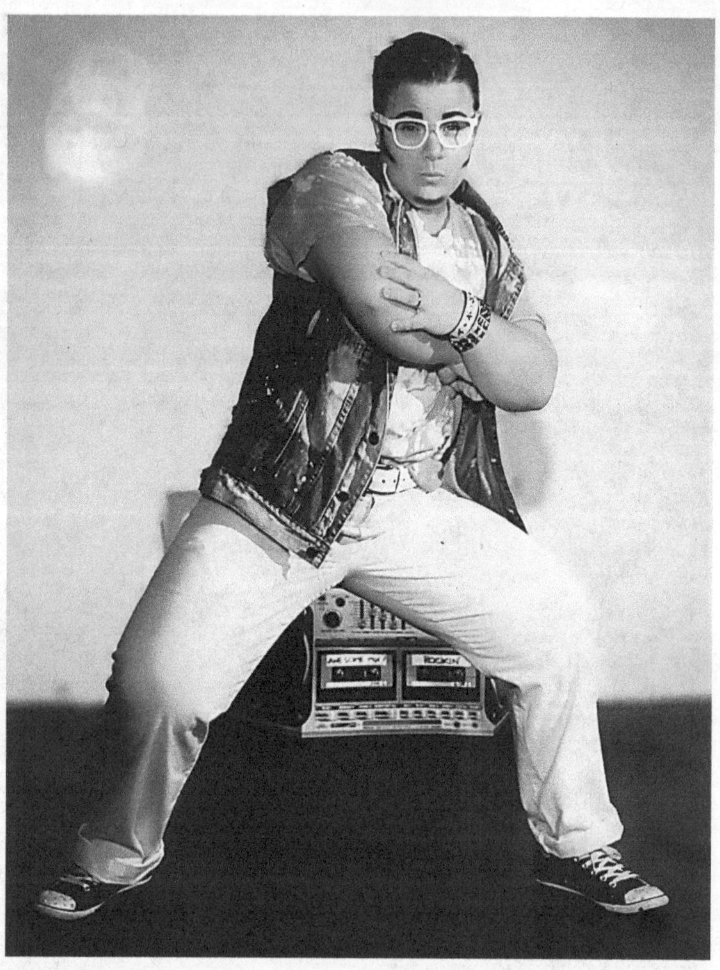

Drag king Trey Alize poses in front of an old stereo in a denim vest and yellow glasses.

2016, Trey's drag career really took off when he won the YouTube reality show competition *King Me: Rise of a Drag King*. Trey said that afterward he was offered a full-time job at Play Dance Bar in Nashville. He also performs weekly at other nearby bars.

Although Trey now works at Play and has a team of other kings he performs with, he admits that the team is "very, very young, and it's been a hard struggle to try to prove ourselves. . . . Since probably about 2008 or 2009 [drag kings] still only have one night that they allow us to be predominantly—to be on stage really. They sometimes will bring a king up for a weekend night, very, very rarely. . . . Other than that, we had one night [or] . . . you have to travel."

Drag Pageant Scene

Another important component for many kings in the South is the drag pageant scene. Drag pageantry models traditional beauty pageants, where contestants must compete in various categories, including talent, interview, formal wear, and so on, to be crowned the winner. Perhaps surprising to some, the first drag pageant in the United States, Miss Gay America, was held in Nashville, Tennessee, in 1972 at the Watch Your Hat and Coat Saloon (Miss Gay America 2020). Today, Miss Gay America is one of the most prestigious and well-respected pageant systems for female impersonators in the world (Miss Gay America 2020).[9]

Though D-Luv Saviyon's knowledge of drag kinging in Nashville started in 1999, he said that other kings had been active in the area since maybe the early 1990s. D-Luv explained, "Mac [Productions] has been doing pageants probably . . . since maybe the late '80s or early '90s. She has always done divas. She lets everyone perform, but her expertise is initially with Mr. Esquire, which is one of the longest running, if not *the* longest running, drag king pageant in the nation, I'm almost positive. . . . Mac is, like, historic. That's who the kings, I think, mostly worked with. If you want to know about the history of drag in Nashville and all about kings and everything, that's your person."

The Mister Esquire Pageantry System, along with its sister pageant, Miss Tennessee Diamond Diva, is part of Mac Productions.

9. For more information about how the drag queen pageant scene developed in one part of the United States, see the book *Drag Queens and Beauty Queens* by Laurie Greene (Rutgers University Press, 2020) about the Miss'd America Pageant in Atlantic City, New Jersey.

Mac Huffington moved to Nashville from Chicago and found an inviting gay community (Grady 2019). When Mac found the pageant scene, they had a vision of making drag kings as popular as drag queens (Grady 2019). With this goal in mind, Mac started Mac Productions to promote drag kings, which began booking drag kings at every show they could find. In 1996, Mac started the Miss and Mr. Nashville Pride Pageant. The following year, Mac started the Mr. Esquire Pageant for Male Impersonators (Grady 2019). The first year of Mr. Esquire, there were thirteen contestants at Connections Night Club in Nashville, and over 200 people were in attendance to watch the pageant (Grady 2019). When Mac began Mr. Esquire in Nashville in the mid-1990s, there were few other pageants in which kings could perform (Grady 2019). Due to Mac's work with the drag pageant scene in Nashville, Trey Alize said, "a lot of people in the South, kings especially, would look towards Nashville . . . because we have a lot of [kings who have] performed in our community that are national title holders. The pageant systems are very big on national titles."

Today, however, there are a number of national pageants for drag kings. Mr. Esquire is one of those, now in its twenty-fourth year. Mac also owns another national pageant, Pageant for Divas, which is open to "all biological females" who are at least twenty-one and is in its fourteenth year (Grady 2019). Mister USofA MI (male impersonator) is another pageant many southern kings have been involved in. This pageant began in 2008 and is "open to all individuals who were born a woman and who are 21 years of age" (USofA 2020). In 2012, Mister USofA MI also began a "classic division" for male impersonators, or drag kings, who are over thirty-three years old.

D-Luv Saviyon got involved in pageants early in their history. He won Mr. Nashville Pride in 2002 and Mr. Esquire in 2006, and was crowned Mister USofA MI Classic in 2013. He said that he "became addicted to pageants." D-Luv explained that many pageants for male impersonators and kings have been started over the years. He said that there are a lot of pageants that take place in Atlanta, including, currently, the Peach State Pageant MI.

Another major pageant for drag kings in the Southeast was Mr. USA Unlimited, which was founded in 1985 in North Carolina. While USA Unlimited began as Mr. Gay USA, for cis gay men, a Mr. Gay USA FMI (female male impersonator) category was added in 2007 and became Mr. Unlimited FMI in 2010. The USA Unlimited Pageants lasted until 2017. Two kings in this study, Teddy Michael (Mr. Unlimited FMI 2016) and Shook ByNature (Mr. Unlimited FMI 2014), won titles in this pageant.

In addition to the national pageant scene, there are a lot of local preliminary pageants around the region that kings must win to qualify to be sent to the national pageant. D-Luv explained the process to me: "For those national pageants, you have to qualify. . . . You go to the prelim, you compete in the prelim, and you win whatever that state's prelim is. Then, from there, you get your ticket to go to nationals. . . . Then, the prelim has a promoter, so the promoter basically pays your way into the national pageant, and they help you along the way as far as your preparation to compete and try to win the national pageant." According to D-Luv, "Drag is always growing." While the local queer bars continue to struggle in the Southeast, D-Luv felt that the pageant scene for drag continues to grow and provide an avenue for kings to perform. However, not all of the kings I spoke with were as pleased with the pageant scene as D-Luv. In fact, Diego Wolf said, "I've only ever done one pageant and that's the only pageant I'll ever do. I freaking hate pageants. . . . That was honestly one of the worst experiences of my life. Much like all pageants are, it was way too much politics and not enough focus on talent, and that's why I don't do them. It's not my cup of tea."

Concluding Thoughts

D-Luv found it encouraging that the pageant scene has gotten a lot bigger for male impersonators and drag kings over the last thirty years. He explained that the pageants continue to add more categories and become more diverse each year. However, he said, as drag becomes more mainstream, the competitions become more challenging:

> There's a lot more places to showcase yourself as a king across the nation. At the same time, I think that drag is falling under what I feel is, in a way, pop culture now because it's become popular and normalized through things like RuPaul, which is still good because people come out to a drag show, but in some aspects is unrealistic because they want what they see on TV and that's not all drag. I think that [it] is important . . . to try to make people understand that there are different aspects of drag, and kings are still not as visible, and divas are still not as visible on the forefront. It's still mostly queens, and I dearly love queens, but everybody deserves a place. Drag doesn't have . . . a limitation to who can do it.

Overall, drag is changing. As *RuPaul's Drag Race* and other shows about queer life become more well known, drag will be influenced by these changes in society. While, like D-Luv, I am optimistic that this will be a positive change for drag kinging, I wonder if bringing drag into mainstream culture will in some ways make it less meaningful to the queer community. I wonder if it will be stripped of its queer roots and revolutionary power if everyone is doing it and watching it.

Roscoe McCoy also brought up *RuPaul's Drag Race* but was not quite as optimistic about its effects as D-Luv. Roscoe said, "In some ways, drag is a dying art form no matter how many seasons of *RuPaul's Drag Race* we've got, because it has always, to me, been a very cutthroat culture that, like I said, even back in the day, if you didn't have somebody to mentor or sponsor or speak for you, you weren't given an opportunity to even get on a stage." Patrick Jacquard also felt that the scene was dying in the Tupelo, Mississippi, and Memphis, Tennessee, regions: "There are absolutely no kings in Tupelo. . . . Memphis, there's probably three that perform."

Most of the performers I spoke with between 2013 and 2019 identified themselves as drag kings. However, a minority preferred different labels and types of performances, such as male impersonator, male illusionist, or "boylesque entertainer." As I mentioned earlier, the line between drag king and male impersonator has been blurred over the last three decades of drag in the United States. While some kings used the terms interchangeably, D-Luv Saviyon had a particular preference for male impersonator. He said, "I am labeled still as a drag king by origin and familiarity, but years ago I adopted male impersonator. I personally feel a male impersonator is someone who has a higher, more polished level of drag. They go further in their craft and are the kings that have you questioning if they are or aren't an authentic born male."

Another change that has occurred within drag kinging, and drag more generally over the last three decades, is that assumptions can no longer, if they ever could, be made about the types of physical bodies the performers have underneath their performances of gender (Sennett and Bay-Cheng 2002). There is a large and growing number of trans and gender nonbinary drag kings in the southeastern United States. Additionally, there are more cisgender people performing the gender that aligns with the sex they were assigned at birth—that is, a cis male-bodied person who performs masculinity as a drag king (sometimes referred to as a "bio king" or a "faux king") or a cis female-bodied person performing femininity as a drag queen (sometimes referred to as a "bio queens" "faux queen," "diva queen," or "hyper queen"). During my observation of drag shows, I witnessed this phenomenon—a female-bodied person performing femininity as a drag queen and a male-bodied person performing masculinity as a drag king.

Diego Wolf told me that today he prefers to perform "boylesque"—a play on the word "burlesque," where performers exaggerate masculinities through their dancing, costumes, and/or striptease. Diego says he splits his time now between drag kinging and boylesque, and that the boylesque scene is a lot more accepting of trans performers. Diego says that more places have burlesque shows now than drag shows around Athens and Atlanta, Georgia, and that there are more opportunities for travel. He described some of the differences between drag kinging and boylesque:

> It's a little bit different than drag kinging, if you will. Of course, I'm kind of a niche performer now because typically in burlesque, lip synching is not common, but I still continue to lip-synch to this day. What I do to the burlesque industry, it's very unique. To drag, while you have your critics that—drag has always had its critics of trans individuals that continue to do drag once they've completed or [are] in the process of transitioning, but that's never interfered with me doing exactly whatever I want to do. . . . [Boylesque] is a whole different type of creative and professional process in terms of how you actually get to the stage.

For Diego, this is a good thing for trans performers especially.

Trey captured these overall changes in southern drag culture well. He explained that "a big part of the drag king history" is that it "started, where it was just mainly cross-dressing, and you're representing the opposite sex of what you are; [on the contrary] nowadays, [being a drag king] has so many different definitions." Trey continued, "[Today] you have trans kings . . . that are still drag kings because they're still presenting drag." Trey said, "Drag maybe back in 2006 and 2007 was a very basic definition of you're a woman representing a man. That's what you're portraying. That is not the way it is in 2019. It is a hypercharacter that you're presenting. . . . You're hyperizing this character that you want to be and you're putting that on a stage, and I think that then the biggest adjustment, the biggest change, the biggest growth of our community is realizing that it can be more than just that one . . . box and definition. That it can be so many different things." He said it no longer mattered what sex you were assigned at birth or identify with. Anyone can perform any gender in drag today. This progressive view of drag was not equally distributed across the kings I interviewed and largely depended the age and location of the interview subject.

2
Drag Kinging at the Intersections of Identities

I met Bo on the patio of PT's 1109 on a sweltering evening in June 2013. Bo seemed nervous about the interview and was not nearly as talkative as most of the other kings I spoke with. He told me he was born and raised near Columbia, South Carolina. His mom worked for a printing press, and his dad was a manager of NAPA Auto Parts. Now, at thirty-eight years old, Bo lives in Columbia and works as an electrician. He said he was never a stereotypical girl: "All I did was play sports and stuff." Bo said his mom always called him a tomboy, but he always *knew* he was a girl. When I spoke with Bo in 2013, he identified himself as a white lesbian woman.

Bo started performing drag about a decade before we spoke in 2003. He said he remembers the year because he was one of the original Cabaret Kings. His friend suggested he give drag a try and said Bo could be the "redneck of the crew." If you heard Bo's southern drawl and saw his dirty, torn-up hat with a big fishhook on the bill, which he said was his trademark, playing the "redneck" of the crew made total sense. In addition to the "redneck," Bo also became "known as the drag king on roller skates." He said he had only performed once without them. The second time he ever performed he wore his roller skates and made a lot of tips, so he decided to perform that way every time. Bo said he performed drag mainly because it is fun: "I do it for fun. I like to go out there and have a good time, show somebody a good time."

Conversely, Rivers Cuomo identified as a white, queer, genderqueer person with a master's degree, and said he performed drag "because gender bending is one of my favorite things in life. Hypermasculinity and hyperfemininity help call gender out as the social construction it is and include a great deal of fun in the process." He went on to say, "Drag is more an expression of the way I have felt about gender since my first courses on the subject in the early 2000s. It certainly provides experiences congruent with the way gender is experienced by others in a more visceral way than you could experience through reading, talking, and theorizing." Rivers, also thirty-eight years old and from South Carolina, was one of only four kings I talked to for this project who held a postgraduate degree. He identified himself as a therapist specializing in gender and sexual identities. Rivers said, "If it weren't for the Internet, or my significant advanced education on the topic of gender, I would be screwed." This advanced education on the topic meant that he was the only king in this study to explicitly define drag as an avenue to point out the contradictions of gender.

Like drag kings themselves, drag king performances have the ability to expose the contradictions and complexities of the performance and categorization of gender (Noble 2002) and other intersecting identities. Specifically, drag kinging exhibits that masculinities are intersectional and do not belong solely to male bodies. To demonstrate how drag kinging can be used as a tool for understanding gender, I utilize the theoretical frameworks of multiple masculinities, manhood acts, and intersectionality.

Multiple Masculinities, Manhood Acts, and the Importance of Intersectionality

Understanding masculinities as multiple and inherently related to other intersecting identities (R. Connell 2005) allows room to think about masculinities not connected to specific types of bodies and personalities. In the United States, masculinity is most valued when it is young, white, male, and heterosexual—hegemonic masculinity (Butler 1990; R. Connell 2009; R. Connell and Messerschmidt 2005; Halberstam 1997, 1998). When masculinities are performed by other people, that person becomes suspect, ignored, or stigmatized. While there are culturally exalted, or hegemonic, ideals of masculinity based on time and place, multiple masculinities theories posit that there is no one form of masculinity that is consistent across cultures and history (R. Connell 2005). Understanding masculinities as multiple allows for an intersectional analysis of how other vectors of privilege and oppression such as race, socioeconomic class, and sexuality can lessen the power and resources available to certain men. While studies of masculinities to date have largely focused on people who were assigned to the male sex at birth—based on the assumption that masculinities are only a property of male bodies—this cisnormative lens for exploring masculinities has left many aspects unexamined.

The difficulty in defining what masculinities have in common led Schrock and Schwalbe (2009) to propose the related concept of "manhood acts." They argue that this concept more precisely defines the issue at the heart of masculinities research, which is *how* men achieve dominance. Schrock and Schwalbe (2009, 281) suggest that "all manhood acts . . . are aimed at claiming privilege, eliciting deference, and resisting exploitation." Clearly, gaining "creditability as a man" and the right to the privileges that this identity bestows is made easier by being born with a male body (Schrock and Schwalbe 2009, 279). To be accepted into the category of "man," one must "put on a convincing manhood act," and having a male body helps to support that act (Schrock and Schwalbe 2009, 279). For people who do not hold identities considered to be hegemonic in our society (whiteness, heterosexuality, able-bodied, etc.), compensatory manhood acts, or exaggerated *performances* of masculinities, are carried out in order to gain dominance and the privileges of masculinity (Ezzell 2012). Without a male body and other identities of privilege, people must engage in behaviors that emphasize their sameness with hegemonic men (Abelson 2016; Sumerau 2012).

Drag kinging provides visual evidence to support theories of multiple masculinities and intersectionality. Most kings understand that there is a hegemonic form of masculinity. However, while some kings use the stage to learn to achieve this hegemonic form, others use the stage to challenge masculinities and demonstrate the performativity of all genders. Shook ByNature, for instance, explained that drag allowed him to "learn how to walk, stand, talk, flirt like a man. . . . Drag made my male illusion flawless." Shook learned through drag how to imitate what our society believes it means to be a man. Raewyn Connell and James Messerschmidt (2005) explain that hegemonic masculinity is always positioned in relation to femininities and subordinated or marginalized masculinities. While Shook identified as African American, a marginalized status in our society, he was sure to position his masculinity as strong in relation to others. Shook explained, "Above all else, I am two things . . . ruthless and a gentleman." He learned this through his research on masculinity, which he described as necessary to "look grand on stage." Contrastingly, Justin Time, a twenty-three-year-old white bisexual male in South Carolina, explained: "Just because someone identifies as a man, it does not mean that man is masculine. Meaning, some men are very feminine, myself included. I enjoy wearing makeup and dressing nicely. That's just who I am, and I want others to know there's no wrong way to be yourself. Makeup is feminine, but it is not strictly female."

In addition to highlighting the pluralities of masculinities, drag also intersects with performers' other identities. Consequently, in addition to gender identities and expressions, drag provides a critical lens for examining how geographical location, sexualities, race, socioeconomic class, age, and so forth, intersect with gender. As Shields (2008, 302) explains, intersectionality allows us to examine how various social identities "mutually constitute, reinforce, and naturalize one another." The concept of "intersectionality" was coined by Black and multiracial feminists to complicate the notion that studying gender or race *alone* allows an understanding of inequality. The intersectional approach moves scholars beyond adding up oppressions, to the consideration of unique standpoints within what sociologist Patricia Hill Collins (1986, 2009) calls the matrix of domination. Further, our geographical location often changes the meanings of these intersecting characteristics (Abelson 2019; Glenn 2002; Mohanty 2003).

To illustrate, Schilt (2006) shows how race and ethnicity negatively influenced trans men's privileges in the workplace. The experiences of trans men of color in the workplace were "markedly different than [those of] their white counterparts, as they are becoming not just men but Black men, Latino men, or Asian men, categories that carry their own stereotypes" (Schilt 2006, 485). Similarly, Abelson (2016) finds that trans men often fit in and gain acceptance in the South and in rural areas of the country by claiming sameness with other men through their identities of whiteness and rural working-class heterosexual masculinities. By being read as a white, working-class, heterosexual man, and not as trans, some of Abelson's (2016) respondents were able to live comfortably and be accepted. However, being seen *only* as men was not an option for men of color, men who presented gender in nonconforming ways, or men who did not identify as heterosexual. These men were not granted the same access to the benefits of masculinity in the South.

Geographical location is a major intersecting characteristic that must be examined when discussing gender but is often overlooked in research. For instance, the meaning of gender and masculinities in the southeastern United States varies considerably from other regions of the country. Accordingly, when many of the kings in this study are performing masculinities, both on and off of the stage, they do so from the perspective of a Southerner. In the southern United States, gender remains constructed in largely binary (male/female and man/woman) and limiting ways. Stereotypical gender performances and expectations continue to be omnipresent and heavily policed in this region of the country. While the South has begun to resemble other regions of the United States in some ways, gender ideology is one of the ways that the region remains distinctly conservative (Reed 2018). For instance, the majority of Southerners continue to believe that men should have more authority than women and that women should primarily take care of the home (Carter and Borch 2005; Reed 2018; Watts 2008).

Overall, multiple masculinities, manhood acts, and intersectionality demonstrate that gender is inherently a category of inequality, and, therefore, "doing manhood" (or any other hegemonic identity) is always about gaining dominance and power (Ezzell 2016). If performing manhood acts is by definition a way to achieve dominance and privilege, then there can be no healthy or inclusive version of manhood. As Ezzell (2016, 195) theorizes, while "it is conceivable to construct and promote healthier masculinity for individual men, in the process we are still reinforcing larger structures of inequality by reinforcing the gender system."

Southern Manhood and Masculinities

In the South, ideals of gender are unique to the region and directly tied to racial history and identity. Historically, being a white man in the South meant holding three core values: honor (the public characteristic or behavior demonstrated through civic identity and nostalgia over the past), mastery (an internal characteristic demonstrated through having control over the household, including wives, children, and slaves), and independence (especially financially, shown by owning your land and not answering to anyone else) (Friend and Glover 2004; Watts 2008). Mastery over slaves, specifically, set southern white versions of manhood apart from white manhood in other regions of the country. After the Civil War, southern white manhood continued to develop along a distinct trajectory related to its racial history.

Once white men in the South could no longer define themselves through mastery over slaves, they set up new hierarchies. Following the Civil War, southern white men became even more concerned about their control over their wives and children. They also justified continued control over Black men in the region under the guise of protecting white women. Collins (2004) demonstrates that during Reconstruction white southern men used false claims of sexual assault against white women by Black men to justify lynching and other forms of violence against Black men. This violence against Black men was "a last-ditch imperative" to save the way that southern white men had constructed southern masculinity (Cobb 2005, 174). In reality, the violence against Black men was aimed at halting any economic, social, or political progress Black people were striving for that white men viewed as a threat to their own success and power in the region (Cobb 2005).

Another distinction southern white men created was to define themselves in contrast to the "urban, industrial, liberal, corrupt, effeminate men of the North" (Friend 2009, x; Watts 2008). Southern white masculinities defined femininity as "the antithesis of, and the greatest threat to manliness" (Friend and Glover 2004, xiii). While women, specifically white women, should be protected, any degree of femininity witnessed among men was viewed as a direct attack on men's right to control and rule. Due to the focus on femininity as the antithesis of manliness, by the early twentieth century, southern manhood also began to be defined as always heterosexual (Friend 2009; Watts 2008). Overall, a southern man is expected to be strong and aggressive, while simultaneously controlling himself and those under his protection, all the time ensuring that no one insinuates he is gay (Friend 2009).

Clearly, Black southern masculinities were greatly influenced by race. In fact, Snorton (2017) demonstrates through literature how blackness and manhood were constructed as antithetical during the times of slavery. Snorton (2017, 105) notes how in 1967 Frantz Fanon described "blackness as an exclusion from the dominant symbolics of gender, which is to say that within an antiblack patriarchal formulation, the black man cannot be a man." Snorton (2017, 119) continues, "In the production of blackness as monolithic and of black people as interchangeable, gender difference continued to be lost." Overall, viewing Black people as possessions, not people, meant that gender was not seen as relevant to those in power and even in many early Black writings.

Drag Kinging: Masculinities, Intersectionality, and the South

Drag kinging challenges the claim that masculinities belong only to male bodies. Despite masculinities research complicating the notion of a static form of masculinity, most masculinities research continues to limit masculinities to male bodies and to ignore the importance of geographic location as an intersecting characteristic. By overlooking masculinities expressed by women, trans people, and nonbinary people, this research "evidences a cisgender and biologically essentialist bias" (Abelson 2019, 15). Additionally, researching masculinities without taking into account place leads to a metronormative bias (Stone 2018). The drag kinging community in the southeastern United States is an excellent site for exploring masculinities where they exist outside of male bodies, both in the performances and in the performers' everyday lives, and in a region of the country often ignored in social science research about queer lives.

Without a male body, or other characteristics of privilege, to back their claims of masculinity, drag kings must learn how to perform a version of masculinity that is accepted. For some scholars, this means that the main difference between drag kings and drag queens is that femininities have always been viewed as performative—something people can do or act out—whereas until recently, masculinities—especially white, male masculinities—were seen as nonperformative—the baseline from which all other gender performances are measured (Butler 1990). As Halberstam (1998, 2) puts it, masculinity in Western cultures has always been about "notions of power and legitimacy and privilege," which becomes known "where and when it leaves the white male middle class body." Consequently, Black masculinities, gay masculinities, trans masculinities, female masculinities, and all forms of femininities are seen as performances measured against the hegemonic ideal of masculinity (R. Connell 2009; R. Connell and Messerschmidt 2005).

Drag kings often use "compensatory manhood acts"—such as appearing strong, in control, and sometimes even degrading women—as a way of establishing their masculine presence on the stage. Drag offers a literal stage to learn how to perform masculinities and also to demonstrate that masculinities are in fact performances. Drag kinging challenges the notion of a static and universal masculinity. It allows the performers and audience members the chance to view masculinities as a socially constructed performance (Butler 1990). Yet, it is often hard for performers to leave the feeling of control and privilege on the stage and feel secure in a masculine presentation that is suspect to others. Therefore, kings' displays of compensatory manhood acts sometimes carry over into their everyday lives.

For example, one king, Shawn Stud, a thirty-one-year-old white bisexual androgynous person in Mississippi, explained that when he was young, he felt the need to exaggerate his masculinity in order to gain respect and privilege. Shawn said, "I used to be really hetero-masculine in the way I dealt with women. . . . Around 18 to 20 [years old] I was definitely what I'd call a 'womanizer.' I have guilt about that time. . . . At a certain point I could see that being a tough guy is actually fucking stupid. I let go of that uber-masculine presentation; it didn't feel good, so I let it go, and that allowed me to move more toward androgyny. I am a more feminine partner [now] because I have had negative feelings about being uber-masculine." Shawn learned that to fully embrace masculinity meant embracing the toxic elements of it. This led him to renounce hegemonic masculinity, what he called hypermasculinity, for a softer and gentler version of masculinity that he understood would be questioned, but felt as he got older that he was "okay with that."

Only a few other kings discussed how they mixed femininities with their presentations of masculinities. Beau Davis, a twenty-seven-year-old white straight trans male and stem in Arkansas, explained that within the queer community "stems are not really accepted. You are either a stud or a femme, not both." But, Beau said, "I accept my femininity, but also know my true stud hood. [Some] days I'm girlie and [some] days very boyish." Shook ByNature also said that he loves "being the best of both worlds. I love the look of surprise when people see that under this king there lies the body of a goddess."

Generally, southern drag kings gain a better understanding of gender through performing drag but differ from other kings who have been previously studied in two primary ways. First, southern kings usually cite individualistic reasons for participating in drag. Second, challenging the gender system is not a primary goal for most kings. Whereas drag kinging in other areas of the country has been shown to be overtly political, with kings often claiming feminist motivations, southern drag kings use drag as a way to escape the gender-rigid environments in which they live. They do not seek to change gender ideology through drag; rather, they each wish to temporarily live outside its boundaries. Nonetheless, drag kinging itself can be viewed as a subversive act that challenges cis men's claims to masculinity and allows kings the opportunity to imagine a differently gendered society. Further, after practicing masculinities in drag, some kings feel more confident to perform masculinities in their everyday lives. People who were not assigned male at birth performing masculinities in their everyday lives can be even more subversive than performing masculinities on a stage for show.

How Drag Kinging in the South Differs from Other Regions

The differences between kings in this study and previous research on drag kinging relates to four primary factors: (1) the unique location of the southern United States (as opposed to Santa Barbara, New York, or other major cities); (2) the socioeconomic background of southern kings and how this relates to feminism and politics; (3) the cultural shifts around queer visibility in the United States (2002–2004 versus 2013–2019); and (4) greater racial diversity in the South and this study sample.

IMPORTANCE OF LOCATION

Notably, most of the drag king troupes and scenes that have been featured in academic research and documentaries to date have been located in urban areas outside of the southern United States, and are often related to specific college and university communities with direct ties to feminist agendas (e.g., Drysdale 2019—Sydney,

Australia; Halberstam 1997, 1998, 1999—London, San Francisco, and New York City; Rupp, Taylor, and Shapiro 2010 and Shapiro 2007—University of Santa Barbara, Santa Barbara, California; Smyth's *A Drag King Extravaganza* [2008; documentary]—Columbus, Ohio; Burton's *Kings, Queens, and In-Betweens* [2017; documentary]—Columbus, Ohio).

Drag provides a lens through which to understand some of the unique aspects of gender in the South. Drag allows a look into the lives of people who society, and often their own families, have turned away because they do not meet the cisgender ideals of masculinity or femininity. Though the South may not be ready for overt challenges to the gender hierarchy, drag provides a safe haven for many people to be themselves and feel comfortable in a culture where traditional gender ideals are based in conservative religion and politics. Southern drag kings understand the conservative culture in which they were raised and do not necessarily set out to make a political statement against it, only to remove themselves from it for a short time.

In terms of their stated motivations for entering the drag scene, many kings claimed to perform "just for fun" or to relieve stress. For instance, King Axel explained: "I think people do drag because it's fun to be someone else; for me it helped me deal with a lot of social anxiety. . . . Drag let me put on this cocky persona and just be someone who didn't give a damn how people saw him or what they thought of him. . . . It was pretty awesome." Along the same lines, Mr. Brightside, a twenty-two-year-old white cis lesbian in South Carolina, said: "I think there are several reasons [people do drag]. It could be for fun, the love of the art, an escape from reality, or them being able to be themselves and who they want to be without judgment. I do it for fun and the love of the art." Southern norms of politeness support the status quo, at least on the surface, and these likely affected respondents' willingness to claim the use of drag as a socially subversive force (E. Johnson 2008). Instead, kings said they largely used drag to meet individual needs, which often involved relieving the stress caused by societal reactions to their gender or sexual nonconformity.

The regional context of the southeastern United States played a major part in the decision of many of these kings to begin performing drag. Although two decades ago Halberstam (1998) argued that drag kinging was a phenomenon that takes place in "cities that never sleep," the kings in this study performed across the southeastern United States, in rural areas, in suburbs, and in smaller cities where Halberstam would have likely been surprised to find these thriving drag king communities. In fact, drag kinging in these areas of the country is more significant and essential than drag in major metropolitan areas where there are thriving queer scenes. The majority of kings I spoke with in the South recognized that they resided in a region with increased transphobia and homophobia. They sought out drag as an escape from the oppressive environment in which they lived their daily lives and used it as a place to individually express themselves and seek support. Most kings I interviewed were not consciously seeking to change or challenge the gender status quo of the region where they lived.

In *Female Masculinity*, Halberstam (1998) argued that characterizing drag as "just for fun" was theoretically uninteresting and without import. However, what Halberstam failed to consider is that living in a place where oppression based on gender and sexuality is rampant, as it is in the southeastern United States or rural areas of the country more generally, describing drag as "just for fun" may be a rational act of self-preservation for some drag kings. As Justin Case put it: "I do drag because it's fun. It's a form of entertainment and fun. It's a form of performance. And if anyone who enjoys attention or enjoys being eccentric and out there, they can really enjoy performing drag. I think that drag itself is a huge part of gay history and gay culture." Having fun and expressing yourself in a nontraditional way in the South can be revolutionary in and of itself.

SOCIOECONOMIC BACKGROUND AND CONNECTIONS TO FEMINISM AND POLITICS

The drag kings in this study did not necessarily have the theoretical knowledge of gender and feminism that may have led other kings to drag as a challenge to the gender system. In this study, eleven kings completed their GED or high school diploma, twenty-four completed some college, twelve obtained an associate degree, nine completed a bachelor's degree, and four received a master's degree. Furthermore, the vast majority of kings worked either in the service industry (e.g., restaurant, retail, guest services) or in a blue-collar job (e.g., electrician, warehouse worker, delivery driver, construction worker). See appendix A for specific occupations of the kings in this book.

Comparing these southern kings to those in previous studies—highly educated activists who perform as a direct political challenge to the current gender system—shows that context matters (Piontek 2002; Rupp, Taylor, and Shapiro 2010; Shapiro 2007; Troka, Lebesco, and Noble 2002). Most southern drag kings did not start drag for political reasons or to overtly demonstrate the social construction of gender. In fact, none of the drag kings I spoke with explicitly claimed to be feminists, and only a few seemed to identify at all with the mission of feminism as a struggle for equality among all genders. Most drag kings from previous research are described as graduate students and individuals who hold theoretical knowledge of the impact of gender and sexuality on society (Piontek 2002; Rupp, Taylor, and Shapiro 2010; Shapiro 2007).

For instance, one troupe was made up of individuals who held "connections to academic feminism and queer theory," which led them to perform "to numbers that conveyed messages about sexism, racism, body size, and militarism, as well as gender and sexuality" (Rupp, Taylor, and Shapiro 2010, 279). Similarly, Piontek (2002, 128) describes a drag troupe engaged in performances that challenge the gender binary; their shows "not only reflect current debates about the performativity of gender in feminism and queer theory; they also complicate them in productive and entertaining ways."

In the southern context, opportunities for progressive change are rarer. Southern kings appear to be aware of this and choose not to fight this uphill battle on behalf of societal change. In the South, making an overt statement challenging gender norms might be unappealing to kings, who live in the same communities ruled by the ideals of politeness and under conservative gender expectations, especially when they perceive that there is little to be gained. Kings already have access to non-cisgender spaces, whether they combine kinging with a political stance or not. Overt protest may feel more like a rhetorical exercise than a set of actions with a practical goal.

Many kings indicated that they had no larger political or theoretical motives for performing drag. These kings were not seeking to change anything but their own lives. When asked if he thought drag kinging was a political statement, Justin Case said, "I can see ways that it would be or could be used like that. But from all the experiences I've had it's just about fun and escape." Similarly, Ayden said that he tries to get his straight friends involved because he feels that they could learn from drag; however, he tries to "get as many people involved that would not normally be involved based on entertainment, rather than making it such a political thing." In general, drag in the South seems to be a tool for individual self-realization, not an explicitly political agenda.

To further demonstrate this point, when I asked drag kings if they thought drag was related to feminism, the majority either did not know what feminism meant or did not see any correlation between drag and feminism. Some had never heard the term or did not know how to define it. Overall, they felt that drag was not an outlet to make a stand for women's equality, and some even felt that drag was the antithesis of feminism. Some kings said that they knew some feminists who did drag or that they supposed it could be related, but no kings claimed to be feminists or to participate in drag for this reason. Wes Starr was one of the kings who perceived a negative relationship between feminism and drag. He said, "I see a negative one, maybe. Given that maybe some feminists look negatively against drag because it is a female trying to be a male, so I think that there may be some negative feelings between that."

Along the same lines, Carson Scott, a forty-four-year-old Native American in South Carolina, questioned how one could be a feminist and trans at the same time. He argued that wanting to transition from female to male exempted the majority of kings from feminism, which he conflated with femininity. Carson said: "How can you be a feminist when you're a drag king? I can't be a feminist and prefer you call me a male while I'm in drag . . . It would be like a hypocrite, like a Bible thumper. Because here I am saying I'm a feminist, I'm all woman, but I'm dressing as a man and wanting you to call me a he. . . . It doesn't go together because a feminist is all woman and all about the female empowerment and everything else and drag kings aren't about that, we'd pretty much rather be not." When I asked Bo what the word feminist meant to him, he said, "God, that's a strong word. To tell you the truth I really don't like that word." I asked him why he did not like the word, and he explained: "Well, the way it feels, I think of that word as hate. I really do. . . . Being a feminist, I wouldn't say you're a man hater, but you put yourself off as that way. The people I've ran into and spoke with they just down-talk men and all men aren't the same."

Finally, Jinx agreed that drag opposes feminism because drag is "an over-celebration of masculinity." These southern kings' understandings of feminism stand in stark contrast to those of kings in studies from other places around the country, whose connections to graduate education meant that they explicitly connected drag to feminism. Unlike West Coast and northeastern kings, who often hold advanced degrees and have been exposed to feminist and queer theory, southern kings, most of whom do not have the same ties to higher education, cannot draw on these tropes when forming their understandings of drag kinging.

While simply having "fun" would suggest that gender norms would be unaffected, I argue that the kings' performances still have implications that go beyond their intentions. Examining drag kinging in the South demonstrates that regardless of the drag kings' purpose for performing—an intentionally political act or not—their performances nevertheless have the potential to challenge the gender system (Willox 2002). That is, opposed to Rupp and Taylor's (2003) argument, I argue that intentionality is *not* necessary for political impact.

By claiming the status of man, even if only for a performance, drag kings question the innateness of masculinity and assert that they have the same right to this power as any other person. Gender norms are thereby challenged when kings perform masculinities in ways that disconnect them from male bodies and reinscribe them onto female bodies, trans bodies, and nonbinary bodies. Because of this, some scholars suggest that drag king performances of masculinities are more revolutionary than drag queen performances of femininities—which according to Willox (2002, 274) merely represent a "comical rebuff to straight society" (Butler 1993; Halberstam 1998). Because masculinity is "assumed to be an origin," drag kinging is always rebellious by pointing out the social construction of masculinities (Halberstam 1998, 279). Hence, if drag king performances are "infinitely more subversive" than drag queen performances, then all drag king performances are "always already subversive whether this is acknowledged by the performer as an intention or not" (Halberstam 1998, 280).

Furthermore, the confidence drag kings gain on stage performing masculinities often translates to performing more masculinities in their everyday lives. For instance, the high proportion of trans men who perform as drag kings in the South demonstrates the potential for drag to lead to true destabilization of the current gender system. By performing masculinities in their everyday lives, trans men, lesbian women, and nonbinary kings rebel against the gender binary system that links masculinities only to those assigned male at birth. The higher proportion of trans drag kings, as opposed to trans drag queens, also demonstrates how drag kinging is highly related to the subversion of the gender system. Kings demonstrate through their performances both on and off stage that gender is not innately tied to biological sex, and at a minimum is a social construct that can be chosen or altered.

That southern kings do not put these challenges into words that are familiar to academics does not eliminate their impact. Regardless of the kings' intentions, their views of gender were transformed through drag. Drag kinging allowed participants to gain a real-world understanding of gender, including that "what's between your legs is totally different from what's in your head . . . than who you are" (Conner Rush Dupri, a twenty-seven-year-old white pansexual female). At the same time, this does not negate the fact that the purposely sexist names, song choices, and performances of drag kings can reinforce power differentials between masculinities and femininities and can reify certain forms of hypersexual, aggressive, and toxic masculinities.

QUEER VISIBILITY AND UNDERSTANDING ONE'S GENDER AND SEXUAL IDENTITIES

A lot has changed for queer people in the United States since the early 2000s, including, but not limited to, more queer representation in the media (including trans representation over the last few years), federally abolishing sodomy laws (2003), changes in how gender identity disorder is discussed and labeled in the medical community and in the fifth edition of the *Diagnostic and Statistical Manual of Mental Disorders* (DSM-5), published by the American Psychiatric Association (2013), legalization of same-sex marriage (2015), and allowing trans people to change identification documents to match their gender identities.

In one of the few studies of drag kings in the United States, Shapiro (2007, 259) finds that drag often "led to participants' gender identify shifts." Shapiro's study focuses on a "feminist drag king troupe" in Santa Barbara, California, in the early 2000s. The kings there found that drag was central to understanding, and often changing, their own gender identities. Shapiro (2007) documented four "collective mechanisms" that led to identity transformations: imaginative possibility; information and resources; opportunities for enactment; and social support. In my interviews with drag kings across the southeastern United States, I found support for each of these mechanisms. However, many of the kings I talked to started drag because they already "felt" that there was something different about their gender or sexual identities or did it "just for fun."

Increased visibility of queer people in everyday life and in the media meant that many of the kings in this study came to drag already exploring or identifying with queer identities. Drag did not lead kings to new gender and sexual identities or to shifts in their identities per se, but rather confirmed their "felt" identities and helped them to put their identities into words. The majority of kings in my study suggested that drag was an outlet for gender and sexual identities and expressions already present but silenced in the broader community. Furthermore, in a region of the country not ready for overt challenges to "traditional" gender and sexual ideals, drag provided kings with a safe haven. Performing was a safe and fun way to test the waters of existing queer identities and allowed kings to question and play with gender and sexuality in ways that were prohibited in their everyday lives.

So, while drag continues to provide space for imaginative possibility, information and resources, opportunities for enactment, and social support, these mechanisms have shifted over time and also look different based on the geographic location of the performers. Drag, as a means to imagine other ways of being gendered and to try on those enactments (Shapiro 2007), remains especially relevant in the southeastern United States, where more conventional gender norms continue to be dominant (Baker and Kelly 2016). While most kings in the South today come to drag with "felt" gender and sexual identities, drag provides many southern kings a space to understand their gender and sexual identities more fully in a supportive environment. As my colleague Kimberly Kelly and I found, "Given the lack of gender transgressive spaces in the South, drag took on an even greater significance in imagining non-cisgender possibilities" (Baker and Kelly 2016, 57).

Nevertheless, the impacts of the imaginative possibility of drag differ based on time and location. In Santa Barbara, Shapiro (2007) found that through participation in drag troupes, the majority of kings either took on a new gender identity or redefined their current gender identity in new ways. In their feminist environment, drag was used to challenge the gender system that the larger American society holds people accountable to, and the kings felt that drag was a place to explore one's own personal gender identity (Shapiro 2007). Shapiro (2007, 251) argued that the process of participating in drag culture functioned as "a form of consciousness raising and a site of identity transformation for performers." Rupp, Taylor, and Shapiro (2010) echo this by suggesting that unlike drag queens, who often question their gender identity at a young age and prior to entering drag, kings often reconsider their own gender identity as a result of performing drag.

While drag was an especially important resource for trans and nonbinary kings, almost all of the kings I spoke with, both cis and trans, explained a long-term identification with masculinities dating back to childhood. Most kings identified as childhood tomboys. As D-Luv Saviyon said, "Yes, I was born a woman, but a tomboy beginning from when I was allowed to dress myself." Yet, the majority of interviewees explained at least some attempt to perform cisgender and heterosexual identities as a result of peer and parental pressure. At the time of their interviews, only about a third of the kings identified as cisgender women (nineteen of sixty) and a quarter (fifteen of sixty) as heterosexual.[10] Of the sixty drag kings interviewed for this study, not a single one identified as both cisgender and heterosexual at the time of their interview. Therefore, the performance of cisgender *and* heterosexual identities that were forced upon most kings, especially during middle and high school, did not align with any of the kings' actual gender *and* sexual identities when we spoke.

Most kings spent their childhood and adolescence in small, southern towns they described as conservative and religious. In these environments, they felt forced to conform to gender and sexual norms. Wes Starr, a thirty-four-year-old white non–gender specific lesbian from South Carolina, explained that he grew up "in a very close-minded part of town, so you couldn't really be out in school. You had to kind of conform to everything around you, so it wasn't like I was going to a high school and middle school in cargo shorts and a polo shirt. I kind of conformed as much as I had to. . . . I still wore blue jeans and tennis shoes and flip flops, but I had my hair long. I wore makeup. I wore kind of girly shirts or t-shirts. As soon as I could join the ROTC I did, because it got

10. All of whom identified as transgender.

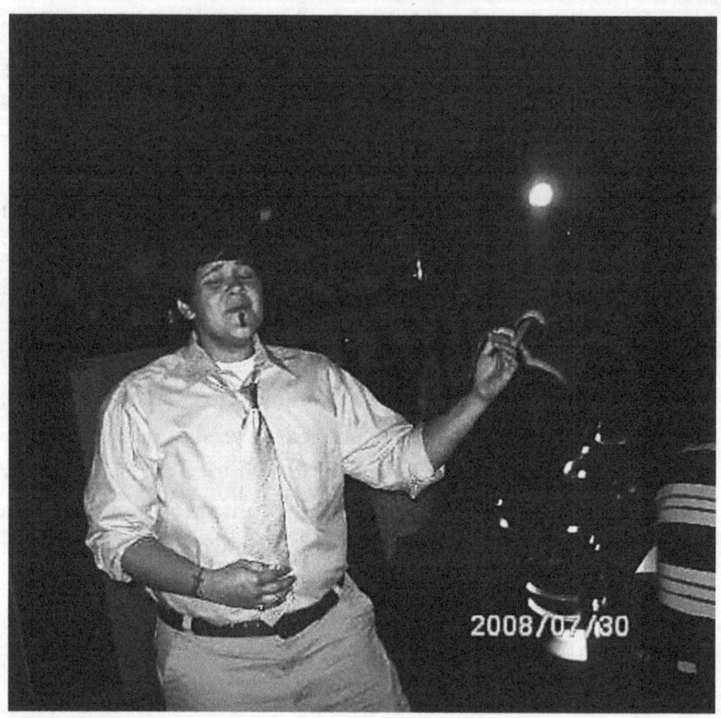

Drag king Wes Starr engages the audience during a performance.

me in uniform, and I didn't have to try and decide what to wear every day."

Although Rider Oliver Fox grew up in Ohio, he also experienced a constricting environment in terms of gender and sexuality due to religion. "While churches and religious communities may often serve as sites of refuge for many," this is often not the case for queer people (Guadalupe-Diaz 2019, 45), especially in the southeastern United States (Rogers 2020). When I asked Rider, who was performing drag in South Carolina when we talked, if he felt that his gender identity had remained constant or changed over the course of his life, he said:

> Constant. That doesn't mean I wasn't pretending. My parents put so much pressure on me, because of my religion, about the

> way I'm supposed to be. . . . I put on a face and I felt very uncomfortable throughout middle school [and] high school life. I had to fit in somehow, so I just was what everybody expected of me. . . . That's why I didn't have a lot of friends . . . people thought I was a freak. They're like, "Make up your mind." I was trying so hard to be something I was "supposed to be." And then my senior year, I finally . . . threw that all away and I was me for once. I wasn't me one hundred percent because I was living with my grandma, which she's sexist and racist and crazy. So, I couldn't do that at my home. . . . I didn't know anything about the drag community, or the gay community. I had no idea about any of that. I just knew who I was all my life. I didn't know there were other people out there like me.

Likewise, Xavier Dupri, a thirty-eight-year-old white straight transgender person, recalled the sense of deception he felt toward his high school gender performances. Xavier, who grew up in small-town South Carolina, explained, "It was all a cover up thing. My family is Southern Baptist. Very religious and it wasn't widely accepted in the middle of the sticks." D-Luv Saviyon said, "I see how judgmental and sometimes hateful people can be. I often ask people opposed to freedom of gender identity what bothers them so much and they usually just call it a sin."

Toward the latter half of high school, kings with supportive friends and family often came out as queer, and some began to transition from a cisgender performance of gender to a more comfortable, masculine self-presentation, such as wearing men's clothing or binding their breasts outside of drag. Nevertheless, most kings had friends and family who were less tolerant of queer gender and sexual identities and expressions, which usually led these kings to delay coming out and adopting more masculine identities until they no longer lived with their families or were financially independent. Unsupportive friends and family are especially detrimental in young people's lives because coming out often leads to major disruptions, and "early disruptions in foundational life stages have the potential to lead to long-lasting consequences, even after some families become accepting" (Guadalupe-Diaz 2019, 41).

For instance, Montana, a fifty-one-year-old white straight man in North Carolina, stated, "I always knew I was a male sporting a lady's body. . . . I always considered myself male but played the female role around my parents so I wouldn't hurt them." When I asked Diego Wolf about his family growing up, he explained, "[My family] knew I was different, but where I grew up at the time transgender wasn't even an idea." Similarly, Andrew Star, a thirty-three-year-old multiracial straight FTM (female-to-male) person in Florida, said that transitioning "was hard since my family did not want to accept who I was. I lost a number of friends because they thought it was ridiculous and strange. I felt more comfortable as I started my transition, but still was extremely depressed because I was hiding the majority of the time."

Importantly, it was not just friends and family who rejected the kings' queer identities; some of the kings turned to drag because of the explicit rejection of their masculine selves or minority sexual identities by peers, teachers, or colleagues. Ivan Eatner, a twenty-six-year-old white straight man, attended a women's college in South Carolina where he did not find much support for his trans identity. Ivan said, "The Provost at my college called me into her office after having my name changed and asked if I had had sex reassignment surgery." The provost told him that she wanted to "make sure I could legally still go to this school." Ivan informed her he had not had surgery and then reported the incident to the dean. Luckily, the provost "no longer works at the college," but this was a very traumatic experience for Ivan. For him, performing drag served as a way to release the stress inherent to his everyday life. Another king, Oliver, was forced out of his sorority when his sisters found out he identified as a lesbian. Feeling isolated and rejected, Oliver Clothesoff began performing drag at a local gay bar as a way to make new friends, noting the tight-knit networks in the drag scene.

Because society gradually became more tolerant and accepting of queer sexuality before really understanding and accepting minority gender identities, kings were more likely to come out as lesbian in high school and college than they were to come out as trans. For instance, Warren Payne, a thirty-three-year-old white Pacific Islander who identified as a lesbian woman, described coming out as a lesbian in high school: "It changed for me my senior year, when I started realizing that I wasn't alone in the way I felt. I felt like liking girls was wrong, but as I started seeing things in the media and around me, I realized that I shouldn't suppress myself to what is socially acceptable and be myself and be in my own skin and feel comfortable." Especially during my initial round of interviews in 2013, media representation of trans people was still largely absent. With limited representation and resources available to trans and nonbinary people, particularly in the southeastern United States, many turned to drag as a venue for expressing a true self that was taboo off stage or used it as a strategy for evaluating whether to transition. Drag provided resources and community necessary for trans and nonbinary kings, who often did not have anywhere else to turn.

Even the kings who identified as cis explained how important drag was as a resource for their friends whose gender identities did not align with the binary. Ayden, a forty-four-year-old white lesbian woman in South Carolina, explained that drag gives his friends who are transitioning a space to be comfortable in their gender identities and expressions. He said, "It kind of gives you a little less limits. . . . I know for several friends who are transitioning, that it is kind of like being able to act out life a little more realistically for themselves." Along the same lines, Jinx, a forty-one-year-old white lesbian woman in South Carolina, said: "I met more transgendered people doing drag than I had ever met before. I guess that's just a natural outlet. I guess more people are naturally drawn to [drag] if they don't feel comfortable in their skin, because it's like the first arena where you're accepted as your new persona." Finally, Justin Case explained the importance of drag as a supportive community, especially for trans people: "Who you are and how you see yourself is . . . very much dependent on who you surround yourself with. So, someone who has transgender feelings, and you're around someone who thinks it's a negative thing and always brings you down, you're always going to hate yourself for it. Whereas, if you surround yourself by people who are supportive . . . just all about it and celebrates who you are, your life will be that much better." Many of the trans and nonbinary kings agreed that drag was a positive environment where their gender identities were celebrated and supported rather than criticized, and this support helped them gain a sense of self-acceptance and locate any resources they needed for gender transition. Being a part of drag culture, especially today, includes having interactions with people of a variety of gender and sexual identities. Due to this, drag culture is a way for kings to connect to resources, information, and social support for addressing their gender and sexual identities, as well as gender transformation. In chapter 3 I focus more on the importance of drag as a space for finding information and resources, opportunities for enactment, and social support for queer identities.

THE SIGNIFICANCE OF RACE

Another important factor in this study that differs from previous research on drag kings is the racial diversity of the kings. As Halberstam (1997, 2018) explains, drag kinging and trans identities have different histories and meanings for white people than for people of color. Race is a key intersectional factor within drag kinging and the queer community. Further, because white and Black lesbian and trans communities developed largely independently in the United States, so too did the ways in which female and trans masculinities took shape within these communities. Specifically, Halberstam suggests that Black female masculinities, and Black drag kings in particular, can be linked to the cross-dressing performances of women blues singers like Gladys Bentley in the early 1900s.

Additionally, race is vital to understanding drag because masculinities of color are viewed as more visible and performative than white masculinities. Halberstam (1997, 112) explains: "White masculinity for the drag king has to be made visible and theatrical before it can be performed, while masculinities of color have already been rendered as visible or invisible, theatrical or nontheatrical in their various relations to dominant white masculinities." For example, people see rapping and dancing as performative, and these styles are linked to masculinities of color, but not to white masculinities. In fact, many white kings initially found it challenging to make white masculinities engaging and exciting because they were seen as so normative. This situation has changed somewhat today, as more white kings are parodying masculinities in ways that may have been more difficult for them to do in the early 1990s.

Seventy percent of the drag kings I interviewed identified as white only, while five kings identified their race as African American or Black, five as multiracial, two as Native American, three as Hispanic, and one each as Pacific Islander, Jewish, and Mexican. While more racial diversity is still necessary to fully understand the dynamics of drag, this study represents a step toward more diversity in queer research with a higher percentage of nonwhite respondents. Other than their racial identities, I did not ask kings about how they thought race intersects with drag specifically. However, some of the kings talked about how their own race or the race of the audience members influenced their performances. For instance, most of the kings who talked about performing country music identified as white, with the exception of Romeo.

When I asked Romeo, a thirty-five-year-old multiracial female lesbian, to tell me about his performances, he said, "I'm Charlie Pride's love child." Charlie Pride is often referred to as country music's first Black superstar. When I spoke with Romeo, he explained that he was the only Black king where he was performing in South Carolina. Romeo said that once people found out that his mom is Black, when they see him perform to "country music [it] is weird." But, he continued, "each king is very different, but it's harmonizing how we all mix. It's like you could do a country number one night or the first half of the show and the second half you know you could go off the wall and do some Manson. It's a chance to transform into something completely different."

Two white drag kings discussed how the racial composition of the audience, often related to the specific bar culture, influenced their decisions on what to perform. Jayden Lee Lowe, a thirty-year-old white lesbian female in South Carolina, explained that each bar he performs at "has a different group you have to appeal to." He went on to explain that at his local drag bar "you have ages eighteen and up, with a wide variety of races and music types and everything." Then, another bar where he performs "is a predominantly Black gay bar," and still another "caters to all races and everything, but has a kinda like very, very even ratio of . . . Black to white there, but more men than women." According to Jayden, all of these intersecting characteristics must be taken into account when you are planning your performance because different types of music and performances appeal to different audiences.

Lucas Storm, who also lived in South Carolina, agreed with Jayden. When I asked Lucas, who described himself as a thirty-year-old white lesbian who also identified as transvestite, if he felt that drag varied based on certain locations, he said that he felt like a lot of the differences were based on the specific bar where the kings perform. Lucas said that depending on the type of bar, the reaction the kings got from the audience would be diverse. He said that when he performed at some shows in Georgia, "the crowd was based on a different race [than white like himself], and I'm not racist at all, but it was based off of a different race, and they give white performers a different reaction depending on the music that they perform. So, I do have to be careful about what songs I perform at different bars. That's basically the only difference." As Lucas went on, it became more evident that he felt he was being judged differently based on his race when he was in the minority in a bar. He explained: "The crowd's reaction is just a little better to somebody of my race. I can perform a variety of different music, instead of having to pertain to just one style. So, I can get a bunch of different genres of music in. It's kind of what I'd like to call a well-rounded bar." The fact that Lucas felt that he could only perform one genre of music if the audience was not white is problematic, but it shows that the presentations of masculinities differ across race, and performers, whether warranted or not, feel that they have to match the type of masculinities they think the audience wants to see to be rewarded with cheering and tips.

Concluding Thoughts

Context and intersectional identities heavily influence drag kinging, leading to variations in how performers understand and perform drag. More conservative gender norms, different educational and employment backgrounds, and lack of media attention to female masculinities all provide a context in which drag takes on a different meaning and purpose for drag kings in the South. Drag provided the kings in this study with personal satisfaction, entertainment, a place for social support, and an environment where it is safe to deal with one's "own [gender] demons" (Xavier Dupri). Even when drag kings participate for fun, drag still has the potential for change. The kings interviewed here and in previous studies gain broader understandings of gender, whether it is their own or gender more generally, which they take out into the world and help to expand its meaning.

Although southern drag kings may not seek to overtly challenge the gender system, as drag kinging becomes more mainstream and accepted, additional people will be forced to reconsider their beliefs about gender. No matter the end goal of drag kings in the South, they are creating change and destabilizing gender. Their performances provide both political and feminist challenges to our current system and demand that our society become more open-minded and accepting of the diversity of gender identities and expressions. It is true that this change will likely occur more slowly in the South and rural areas than in progressive environments or in places where drag is constructed as an explicit challenge to cisgender hierarchies. Nevertheless, southern drag kings play an important part in overcoming the gender hierarchy in our society, particularly in contexts where few other challenges so thoroughly interrupt gender binaries.

3

Drag Kinging as a Resource for Everyday Life

Justin Time was fourteen years old when he came out as "female-to-male transgender." He was scared to come out, because he still was not even fully sure what it meant to be trans, so he tested it out on a few of his close friends first. Justin said that at first he "didn't even know what the word 'transgender' was. I thought I was just confused or sick." After a lot of research and some time, Justin said he began to accept himself for who he was, a bisexual male. Looking back on his childhood, he said, it all makes sense to him: "My brain is wired to be male. I am a boy."

Justin Time came out to his parents at sixteen. His parents were not accepting, and he said he "lost what little bond I had with my mother." He was forced to live on his own after coming out at sixteen and had "no help from anyone other than my loving and supportive friends, who have encouraged me to be who I really am regardless of what other people say." When I asked Justin if he had experienced other discrimination, in addition to family rejection, due to his trans identity, he responded, "Is water wet?" For Justin, high school was especially bad, and he told me a story to illustrate.

Justin wanted to participate in "the masculine equivalent to a beauty pageant" at his high school. First, the principal told him he was not allowed to participate, but he petitioned, and eventually the principal gave him the go-ahead to participate. Once he was granted permission, though, he started facing pushback from "several cis gendered boys, who were also in the pageant, who didn't like the fact that I was doing it." One of the cis boys' parents called *Live 5 News* in South Carolina, "claiming it wasn't right that a 'girl' was allowed to participate in the pageant," and they picked up the story. The school ended up canceling the pageant altogether after the attention they received from this media parade.

In this chapter, I focus on the drag kings' gender identities and expressions outside of their drag performances. Particularly, I examine how the kings perform masculinities in their everyday lives, the consequences of these performances, and how they use drag kinging as a resource to learn about and get support for gender and sexual identities that do not align with society's expectations. Despite kings' professed lack of political intention for performing drag, and regardless of their own personal gender identities, most kings I spoke with viewed drag as a vital resource for information about gender identities and gender transition for trans and nonbinary kings. The trans and nonbinary kings in this study specifically discussed two main reasons for performing drag that have implications in their everyday lives outside of the performance of drag itself (Rogers 2018). First, they explained that drag was a resource for understanding their existing, or "felt," gender identities. And, second, they said that drag provided them with community support that was often lacking in their daily lives.

Heightened Homophobia and Transphobia Make Drag a Necessary Resource in the South

Just as masculinities are specific to the South, so too are the heightened homophobia, heteronormativity, and transphobia in the region (Barton 2012; Bradford et al. 2013; Mathers, Sumerau, and Cragun 2018). Trans and gender nonbinary people continue to face staggering rates of discrimination, violence, homelessness, unemployment, poor mental health, and suicidality across the country (Bradford et al. 2013; Grant et al. 2011; James et al. 2016; A. Johnson 2015; Mayer et al. 2008), and these negative outcomes are even more pronounced for trans people in the South (Abelson 2019; A. Johnson and Rogers 2019; Rogers 2020; Sumerau and Cragun 2018).

Unfortunately, this leaves many queer people without necessary protections and resources to carry out their everyday lives (Barton 2012; A. Johnson and Rogers 2019; Rogers 2020). Many queer people find it difficult to locate basic necessities, especially specific resources related to their gender identities. Lack of protection, resources, and support increases negative health consequences, leads to increased levels of fear, and exacerbates other structural barriers that contribute to decreased life chances for queer people. As Guadalupe-Diaz (2019, 27) eloquently states, "Overall, trans people live in what can be described as a 'trans-antagonistic' culture, an overtly hostile and oppositional social environment that regulates, polices, and maintains recognition of only two genders." From overt violence and discrimination (Lombardi et al. 2001; Miller and Grollman 2015) to daily microaggressions—"subtle verbal or nonverbal insults directed toward people based on their belonging to a marginalized group" (Nadal, Skolnik, and Wong 2012; Sue 2010)—to the denial of resources (Bradford et al. 2013), those who live outside of the gender and sexual binaries continue to be systematically oppressed. This oppression continues to be amplified in the South.

When I asked the kings in this study about prejudice and discrimination, most of them had dealt with issues outside of drag. Andrew Star explained that he felt discriminated against and harassed at work. Even though his "company accepted and acknowledged [his] transition discreetly," he said, "at work [his transition] was a joke." He explained that his co-workers would "look up my past and spread it around the office, about me not being a real guy." Regarding family, Shook ByNature said, "I've had people question how I can be a good mother to my son if I look like a man." Bastian Sage, a twenty-seven-year-old white straight trans man in Tennessee, explained, "Every day I have people still call me 'she,' knowing I am trans." Roscoe McCoy was accused of only identifying as masculine in order to "do business in a 'man's world.'" And Beau Davis said he faced "discrimination in stores and in public restaurants," and when he tried to correct people they would respond, "Oh, well, you know what I mean" or "I know what you really are." While these may appear to be minor incidences of prejudice, microaggressions can have extremely negative effects on the quality of life experienced by oppressed groups (Sue 2010). Microaggressions add up over time and create unequal conditions for queer people. The kings I talked with understood microaggressions to be clear signals of society's perceptions of them and indications that their humanity was not fully accepted or respected.

Approximately a quarter of the trans and nonbinary kings I interviewed mentioned incidents of prejudice or discrimination at work. They said they lost job offers, were overlooked for promotions, and were fired based on their gender identity. This was especially an issue for some kings prior to their legal documents being updated to show their correct name and gender marker. When applying for most jobs, at minimum you must present some form of legal identification, such as a driver's license. For some jobs, background checks are required, as are birth certificates, which complicates the hiring process even further for trans and nonbinary applicants. For instance, Diego Wolf explained, "I have lost job offers because of background checks prior to legally changing my gender." Matt Mixer, a thirty-one-year-old white straight male in Tennessee, also found it "difficult to apply for job promotions when all the legal documents haven't been changed yet." He said that he had to "transfer departments at work because of the way people talked down to [him] when they found out [he] was trans."

In my book *Trans Men in the South: Becoming Men* (Rogers 2020), I discuss the legal name change process in detail and the burden this effort places on trans men in the South. Each state has different laws for the process of changing your name and your gender marker on legal documents, such as your driver's license and birth certificate. If you were born in a different state than where you live, you have to learn at least two states' laws (in order to change your driver's license in your current state and your birth certificate from your state of birth), as well as federal laws if you want to change your passport, Social Security card, or any other federal documents. Clearly, these laws impact trans and nonbinary people's life chances, potentially forcing those without resources to go by or carry their dead name and the sex they were assigned at birth for the rest of their lives. Some states, like Georgia, require that you publish your name change in a newspaper for a month. In other states, like South Carolina, you are required to get fingerprinted, have a background check, and then appear in front of a judge in an open court. In the end, the process can cost hundreds of dollars and a lot of time and resources. It's often a catch-22: you cannot get a job or promotion without the name and gender marker change, but you cannot afford the name change and gender marker change (in the states where this is even legal) without a job.

In addition to microaggressions and institutional discrimination, some kings also reported overt harassment to the point of physical violence. For example, Skyler D. Light had been "harassed many times on the street or in bars. . . . I've been jumped, dragged out of bathrooms, and had beer bottles thrown at me. I have been followed and verbally harassed." Ryder Cox also experienced overt harassment. He explained, "I have had several instances of discrimination and/or prejudice because of me being transgender. Most are random strangers who either mumble about it or are drunk jerks in a bar. I've had one group of people who got violent years ago, and that was when I realized I'm not invincible. I tend to not be as open about [being transgender] in unfamiliar places or around unfamiliar people [now]." Over time, microaggressions, institutional discrimination, and overt harassment and violence lead to poorer health outcomes and decreased self-confidence and esteem for trans and nonbinary people (Miller and Grollman 2015).

Despite the discrimination and the lack of legal protections, resources, and support in the South, over a third of queer people in the United States live in this region (Stone 2018), including over 500,000 trans people who call a southern state home (Flores et al. 2016). To look at one specific example in the South, the state of Georgia is estimated to be home to over 356,000 LGBTQ adults (approximately 4.5 percent of the state population; Movement Advancement Project 2020) and 55,000 trans residents (Flores et al. 2016). Georgia has the fourth highest percentage of trans residents of any state in the country, and the highest percentage of any southeastern state (Flores et al. 2016). Yet, Georgia is almost completely lacking in protection for queer residents, and actually has laws that prohibit equality for queer people in employment, housing, and other areas of life.

According to the Movement Advancement Project (MAP) (2020), which describes itself as "an independent, nonprofit think tank that provides rigorous research, insight and communications that help speed equality and opportunity for all," Georgia scores a negative 2 out of 38.5 points on their sexual orientation and gender identity policy tally. The "policy tally" for each state "counts the number of laws and policies within the state that help drive equality for LGBTQ people." These include policies on LGBTQ relationship and parental recognition, nondiscrimination, religious exemptions, youth, health care, criminal justice, and identity documents. This means that while Georgia is home over 350,000 queer people, it is one of only thirteen states, most of which are also in the southeastern United States, that have a negative overall policy tally for sexual orientation and gender identity. Clearly, place matters in the lives of queer people.

Drag provides an outlet to escape the unreceptive environment that trans and nonbinary people must navigate in their everyday lives in the South (Kosciw, Greytak, and Diaz 2009; Sinnard, Raines, and Budge 2016). The drag community is frequently one of the few places (or the only place) to turn to for information about gender and sexual identities outside of the binary, as well as gender transition–related questions. Many trans and nonbinary people turn to drag to help them navigate the hostile landscape of gender normativity and transphobia in the Southeast. This is also why, as Drysdale (2019, 29) argues, "Attention needs to remain focused on understanding the specific time and place in which cultural identities are claimed."

Drag as a community support is especially vital due to the limited resources for trans and nonbinary people's mental health and well-being, especially in the South (Benson 2013; Bishaw 2014; James et al. 2016; A. Johnson and Rogers 2019; A. Johnson et al.

2020; Lerner and Robles 2017; Rogers 2020; Shipherd, Green, and Abramovitz 2010; Stroumsa 2014). A growing body of research (Bariola et al. 2015; Bockting et al. 2013; Budge et al. 2013; A. Johnson 2019; A. Johnson, Gibson-Hill, et al. 2020; A. Johnson and Rogers 2019; Testa, Jimenez, and Rankin 2014) demonstrates that community involvement and peer support among trans and nonbinary people enhance mental health experiences and moderate some of the negative effects of stigma and discrimination. For instance, Bariolo et al. (2015) demonstrate the positive influence of frequent contact with other queer people on trans people's development of resilience. They argue that "for marginalized people, identification with similar others allows for the development of a positive in-group identity, encourages positive self-appraisal, and allows access to group-level coping" (Bariolo et al. 2015, 2112). Similarly, Testa, Jimenez, and Rankin (2014) show that when trans people start to explore their gender identities, as many of the kings in this study did through drag, having an awareness that other trans people exist and engaging with other trans people greatly enhance psychological well-being. The importance of interaction with other trans people is so vital that one study found this interaction cut suicide rates in half (Testa, Jimenez, and Rankin 2014). Finally, in my work with Austin Johnson (2019), we demonstrate how community support and involvement with a trans community organization in the Southeast enhanced the emotional and psychological well-being of trans and nonbinary people by normalizing trans identities and experiences, creating a social support network, and empowering trans people.

Unfortunately, there are few trans and nonbinary community support organizations in the South. Although many kings discuss drag as a form of entertainment and fun, more importantly drag serves the role of providing a community support organization for trans and nonbinary people in the South, often in rural areas where no other resources exist. Many of the trans and nonbinary drag kings in this study used drag as a resource to examine their "felt" gender identities and to begin to live comfortably in that identity, especially in those areas outside of the few major cities in the southeastern United States (such as Atlanta, Georgia, where resources are more abundant, but still not comprehensive). For instance, Ryder Cox, a thirty-two-year-old Native American and white straight trans male in South Carolina, said that drag provided him with a space where he could be himself "without fear of judgment," a space where non-cisgender identities were not only accepted, but also celebrated. The stage offered him relief in a region were stigma continues to be associated with non-cisgender and non-heterosexual identities.

Drag provides resources for queer people to test some of the social constructions we have been forced to live with in this conservative region of the country. Through drag, we play with gender, sexuality, race, class, and many other constructs that have limited our lives in ways that others may feel are normal and healthy, but to us often feel constraining and suffocating.

Drag as a Safe Space to Explore Gender

Most trans and nonbinary kings I spoke with came out to others as trans or gender nonbinary *after* starting to perform drag. For example, Johnny Walker, a twenty-seven-year-old white Hispanic male from Georgia who started performing drag when he realized he was trans, said, "Performing as a drag king just affirmed the fact that I felt better expressing myself as male and I was even more outgoing." After he became comfortable with himself, he said his friends also accepted him.

The trans kings in this study felt that drag helped them with their gender transitions. While nearly all of the trans and nonbinary kings knew they felt different with regard to their gender throughout their lives, drag kinging provided them with an arena to begin to understand and accept their "felt" identities and to transition into the person they wanted to be. Ryder Cox came out to himself as trans before he began performing as a drag king, but eased others into his gender transition through drag. He explained, "It was a lot easier to ease people into seeing me the way I see myself after they either see a performance or know that I am a king." For

Ryder, drag kinging "was a way to be exactly who I wanted to be. . . . I feel completely comfortable, because I am being viewed as the guy that I know I am." Likewise, Hayden Lowe said, "Performing also helped me figure out who I am as a person and allowed me to mesh Hayden with [my everyday self] to become a better person."

Drag allows kings space to explore their gender identities and expressions and become more comfortable performing masculinities in a supportive environment. Prince Dryden, a thirty-five-year-old white lesbian female in South Carolina, noted that drag "helps me to express myself in a way that I can't necessarily muster up the courage, or have the self-confidence to be in everyday life. . . . [On stage] my whole demeanor changes, my whole outlook about the way I feel about myself changes." Other kings struggled to come to terms with their masculinity, and the reinforcement offered by performing masculinities in a positive atmosphere made negotiating gender easier, as Lucas Storm pointed out: "I know a few performers do it for the money. Some performers, it's a hobby. Me personally, I do it because when I first started doing drag, I had a really low self-esteem; I didn't really like the way I looked; I didn't really like who I was. I wasn't comfortable with myself. So, when I did drag thinking I was Lucas, I would always feel comfortable. I've always felt comfortable as being Lucas and it's helped me with my own self-esteem." The ability of drag to provide a safe space for exploring gender identity and expression is especially important for trans and nonbinary kings.

Hayden Fury, a twenty-eight-year-old white queer FTM (female-to-male) person in Georgia, described that after he started performing as a drag king, he realized that he was "more comfortable in drag than who [he] was portraying to be outside of drag." Relatedly, Skyler D. Light, a thirty-two-year-old white queer trans male in Georgia, explained, "I knew I wanted to transition before I even started drag, but I needed guidance and a slow/steady path to explore my identity." Drag is viewed as gender play by many kings, whereas gender transition (especially medical transition) is seen as more serious. Outside of drag, there does not appear to be another safe space in the South for a person, particularly an adult, to figure out how they want to perform their gender identity. As Andrew Star put it, "[Drag] helped since I got to express the guy I was, that no one usually got to see. I felt liberated."

For many kings, drag was the first, and often only, place they could be themselves and express their felt gender and sexual identities safely. While a few nonbinary kings discussed "gender identity shifts" (Shapiro 2007), most trans and nonbinary kings felt that they had always identified as a gender that did not align with the biological sex they were assigned at birth, even if they did not have the proper language to explain it from the start. These kings explained that rather than a shift in their gender identity, they were able to *discover* their identity, put it into language, and learn how to feel confident in that identity through drag. Roscoe McCoy said, "I don't think [drag] has changed how I think about gender, but maybe just provided an avenue for me to find a safe space and comfort in my own gender expression and identity."

Other kings referred to drag as their "safe zone." LJ Taylor Fury, a thirty-two-year-old white queer FTM person, clarified, "For me, [drag] was always a dream, and me being trans, performing became my home. I felt the most myself when I was in drag. So, it was, and still is, a creative outlet, as well as, therapy for [gender] dysphoria." Through drag, Montana said, "people could see me on the outside as the man I knew I was on the inside." Drag kinging helped him take the next steps toward medically transitioning his body to match his identity. At the time of the interview, Montana was three years into his medical transition. He explained: "My body was like a car you always wanted. Everything was in wonderful condition but needed some body work and a paint job. Sometimes the outside will make things seem less than the worth. Not sure if this makes sense. But like that old car, until I made the outside as great as the interior and motor, people overlooked its worth. A nice paint job and body work is what people see first, and because I was shy, I needed to be okay and comfortable with a nice shine. Just washing and waxing couldn't do it." Like Montana, other trans kings echoed that drag allowed them to solidify their decision to medically transition and decide what that meant for them.

Papi Chulo, a twenty-eight-year-old Mexican pansexual trans male in Tennessee, described it this way: "[Drag] helped a lot. In many ways, I felt more comfortable being Papi Chulo than I did in my everyday life, because being in drag and being male up on stage gave me a freedom—made me feel normal—I felt like myself. . . . I have to go through this in order to be the man I want to be. . . . [Papi] gave me a lot of life lessons. . . . [Drag] made me realize that I am a man trapped in a woman's body." Or as Brad Night, a forty-three-year-old white straight man, put it, "Doing drag was a springboard for transitioning. . . . It helped my confidence and made the transition seamless."

Drag Kinging as Masculine Socialization

Since none of the kings in this study were socialized as men from childhood, they used drag kinging as a way to learn and try on various types of masculinities. Drag provided kings "a space where they began to imagine other ways of being gendered in their everyday lives" (Shapiro 2007, 260). For trans kings, drag provided space to understand what kind of man they wanted to be and how they wanted to perform their own masculinity. For this reason, many kings used drag as a testing ground for masculinities and learning to "signify masculine selves" (Schrock and Schwalbe 2009, 281). According to Schrock and Schwalbe (2009, 282), "Learning to signify a masculine self entails learning how to adjust to audiences and situations, and learning how one's other identities bear on the acceptability of a performance." This can be especially difficult for trans men who were not born with male bodies to back up their claims of masculinity. Skyler D. Light said, "Drag was my stepping-stone [to my trans male identity]. It helped me pick my name, become comfortable shopping for male clothes, and overall helped me realize my true identity and what made me happiest." For Rivers Cuomo, "Doing drag helped me access parts of my own masculinity and made masculinity more accessible to me, generally."

Given the lack of gender-transgressive spaces in the South, drag took on an even greater significance in imagining non-cisgender possibilities. Some southern kings who wished to transition from female to male bodies used drag as a way to imagine their lives after the transition. Drag helped them to decide if transitioning was the right decision for them, or to imagine living as a man if there were barriers that kept them from physically transitioning. Drag also gave kings the opportunity to make comparisons between their lives and statuses as women and the potential change a masculine identity afforded. Xavier Dupri said that "doing drag gave me the opportunity to experience life as a boy and how society and people react to you as a boy. When you're the only one who knows the truth about what's underneath your clothes, no one else knows, and the way people react to you is so much different. Maybe it's because we're in the South, the Bible Belt or whatever, but it seems like if people think you're a boy you get more respect than if you're a butch lesbian, I guess. So, it was a good start for me to see what life was like looking through someone else's eyes." Likewise, Romeo explained that drag is "a chance to be something [else] for just a minute. . . . Before discovering that I really dig being a guy, it was a chance to be a guy."

Performing masculinities on stage also allowed kings to gauge their performances of manhood in front of an actual audience. Drag facilitated kings' gender transitions by allowing them to test out manhood acts in a safe environment, and in a way that they could still distance the "act" from themselves if it did not go over well. Diego Wolf explained how gender transition is a long learning process. He described drag as the "most common step one of [gender] transition." Diego said, "The assimilation into a life presenting as anything other than your birth-designated sex is utterly *terrifying* [his emphasis]." Because of this, he believed, "Naturally, people gravitate toward an environment that deviates from rigidity. In terms of gender, drag is equivalent to kindergarten." Drag is a space to learn the basics of gender, and even literally play dress-up.

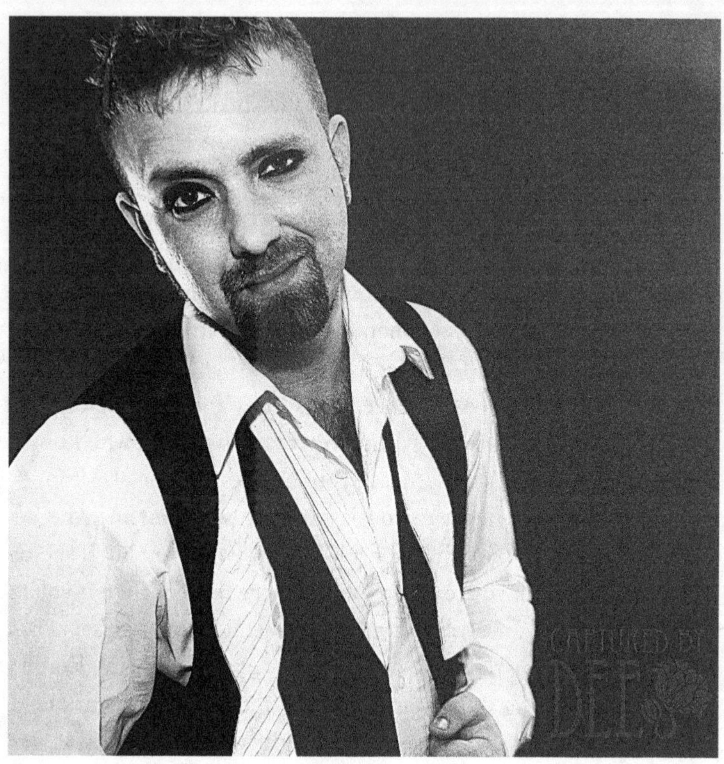

Drag king Diego Wolf grins at the camera wearing an untied bowtie.

Drag as Family and Community Support

Drag provides many kings with a social support system that they do not have access to outside of drag. This support system helps them deal with incidences of prejudice and discrimination. Some kings referred to their drag king networks as families. Rejection by biological families may spur a search for alternative family, or what Weston (1997) refers to as "families we choose." As LJ Taylor Fury put it, "I have learned the true meaning of family and have come to realize that family is not always blood." This analogy to drag families, rather than troupes or casts, seems to be U.S.-centric and largely concentrated in the South. This could also be related to the higher proportion of African American/Black performers in this region of the country and their ties to ball culture.[11] More research is needed to fully understand the intersections of race, region, and drag families.

What I learned about drag families from the kings in this study is that drag families are typically started by experienced performers who mentor newer performers, a process referred to as "raising" them, as one would a son. Hayden Lowe explained that his drag father took him "under his wing and showed me how to do this and how to do that, and basically how to become a king, how to become an illusionist." Then he "fathered" other kings by teaching them how the shows work and how to perform. Frequently, "baby kings" adopt the "daddy king's" stage last name; thus several kings have the same last name, like Xavier Dupri, father, and Conner Rush Dupri, son, in this study. Drag families take pride in being heterogeneous. Specifically, the drag families in my research were racially integrated and emphasized diversity. Many of the white kings had Black drag mamas or wives and racially diverse brothers and sisters. The families were also open and accepting of various gender identities and sexualities. For example, one "brother" might have a feminine appearance outside of drag while supporting another who was in the process of gender transition. Drag family ties persevered even if a king stopped performing or moved away. The depth of these relationships is suggested by the use of a king's real name off stage; family members knew each other well enough to use these names, which are considered private and never used in a performance context; thus more casual acquaintances, such as bar friends, never had cause to use them.

Carson Scott described the drag family system in detail: "I'm actually in the Unlimited Family. . . . The Unlimited is like a big family. Because it's mostly the pageantry system. You know you have so many different groups of different pageantries." In addition to his pageantry family, he said that he has also "run with a

11. Ball culture refers to an underground queer community of Black/African American and Latinx people, many of whom identify as drag queens, who compete, or "walk," on the runway for prizes.

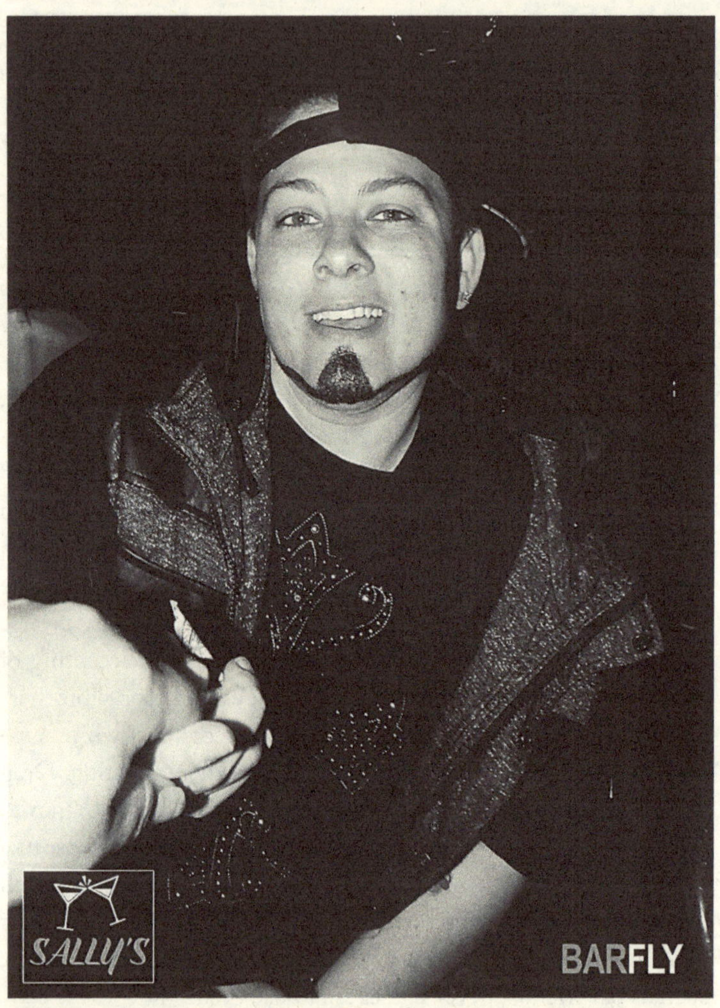

Drag king Hayden Lowe accepts tips as he performs.

few of the Dupris . . . [and he's] actually a Sinclair." However, Carson said he does not use the last name Sinclair "for the simple fact that in order to take someone's name you have to agree with everything they do." Carson went on, "I mean I had no choice when I had to take my [biological] parents' name, because that's my parents, but as an adult I can choose, and if I don't agree with everything they do, I don't feel like I should carry their name." Carson said by keeping his own last name, he can distance himself from any negative press associated with the Sinclair family. He explained: "I don't wanna be associated with that in case it hurts my career. If something happens with my name right now, the only person that could do that is me. So, it's kinda like you only have to answer for what you do, not what everyone else does." Just as with birth family names, Carson is afraid he will become associated with anything that goes on in his drag family. By having a different name from the rest of his family, he is able to keep some individuality and avoid any negative repercussions that families can have.

Despite Carson's reservations about drag families, he did feel they provided important support for himself and other drag performers. Carson said, "I have to say they actually are like a family." He explained that if a family member was in need, someone always stepped in to help. Carson went on, "I mean they're an actual family. There's a mama, there's a daddy, there's sons, and they actually take [their drag children] under their wings." Carson offered an example of "one little king" who had gotten himself into trouble, and relayed how that king's family helped him to get "back on track, and they were pretty much on his case to where he is straightened up now and is doing very, very excellent."

Ryder Cox also belonged to a drag family in South Carolina. Ryder explained: "I do know one big thing that I've experienced in drag is the family of it. Like, my name being Ryder Cox is because an older performer who has been doing it longer and has made a name for herself came to me and said, 'Hey, would you like to be my drag son?' And while that doesn't sound like much, basically what it does is when I come out now, because her name is Carla Cox, when I come out now as Ryder Cox, I'm associated with her. So, everything that I do and the way I represent myself is also representing her." Like Carson, Ryder said that drag families are like birth families. If "as a kid you go out and do something, say illegal, it's going to reflect on your parents too, regardless of whether it should or not." Ryder explained that it is an honor to be asked to join a drag family: "Once you make a name for yourself and you're doing well, and a superior king or queen asks you to be their son or daughter or whatever the case may be, it's an honor. It's almost like a title, like winning a competition."

Ryder said that he does not have any drag children yet, because he has not "found someone who I would like to carry my name like that." He said being in a drag family is an honor, but also a responsibility: "It's a respect issue and it almost, it pushes you to perform better and to put more into [it] because you're not only representing yourself anymore, you're representing your entire drag family." As in birth families, relationships also vary among members. When I asked Ryder if he had a drag dad, he explained that Carla did have another king she called his stepdad but went on to say their relationship was "not as serious as me and her and my sisters. We all carry the same name; we all are very close knit outside of the bar as well."

Xavier Dupri, a member of a multigenerational family in South Carolina, described the close-knit bonds some drag families developed: "Drag families are very much like any normal family." Although he said that "having a drag father is not very common in the upstate," it is actually very "normal" also, considering that 41 percent of families in South Carolina are headed by a single parent (Kids Count Data Center 2020). Due to the smaller number of drag kings in South Carolina, and hence fewer drag fathers, Xavier Dupri said, "most of our influence up here is drag queens. Like, my great grandmother is the national title holder. My grandmother is a national title holder. My mother is a national title holder. And now my son is a national title holder. And we all just stick together under the Dupri name and like represent for each other. We help out a lot with each other's shows and stuff."

Xavier said it was not just on stage that families helped each other out; off stage they are also "really involved with each other's lives." Xavier himself had five drag sons and four drag daughters, and they call each other multiple times a week to check in. He provided some examples of things they have done for each other as a family: "We helped one find a job and get his life back together. We got one of them off of drugs. . . . We keep the boys straightened out. With drag, it's really easy. There are positive relationships in drag, and a lot of times being an entertainer you get steered into the world of drinking and drugs, stuff like that. So we try to keep their heads straight, keep them focused on what exactly they want." Xavier Dupri's statement demonstrates the rewards of belonging to a family both on stage and off.

I also interviewed one of Xavier Dupri's drag sons, Conner Rush Dupri. Xavier saw Connor in a talent show and started giving him advice on performing. Eventually, Xavier took Connor under his wing. Conner said, "Drag actually is really much like a family. Like, there's no doubting that. I feel like they treat me as though I'm their son or I'm their brother. Like, there's no difference in drag family and real family in my opinion." Conner Rush Dupri said his drag family had family dinners most Sundays. Even after he started taking a break from performing, he said, "my drag dad and my grandma still call me and check up on me. It's like even though they know I'm taking a break or may possibly not [be] doing drag, they still call me, and they still check up on me. And when I was doing drag, they'd wanna know what show I was doing, what numbers I was performing, did they need anything to help, that type of thing."

In addition to drag families, many trans and nonbinary kings found the social support provided by the drag community in general to be essential. As Matt Mixer stated, drag helped him "have a bigger support system of people who understood what [he] was going through and who were always there for advice." While other friends and family may empathize with the experiences of trans and nonbinary individuals in the Southeast, only those living through the experience can truly understand the consequences of routine prejudice and discrimination on trans and nonbinary lives.

While creating community support may not be the explicit goal, drag kinging has filled a major gap in resources, especially surrounding the mental health of trans and nonbinary Southerners. Because many trans and nonbinary people cannot access traditional mental health services due to lack of insurance or financial support, and many fear accessing these services (if they can afford them) due to prior discrimination or horror stories they have heard about these services, participating in drag to gain a community of support may be the only option available for many trans and nonbinary kings. Clearly, these issues also relate to health care more generally, which is a resource many southern kings also do not have access to.

Drag as Access to Health Care and Resources

For both cis and trans kings in my study, drag provided them with information and resources about gender identity, and for many it changed the way they thought about gender as a whole. Southern drag kings used drag culture as an educational venue for learning about gender and trans issues. For Justin Case, drag opened his eyes to the possibilities of gender: "[Drag] exposed me a lot to other people, and then doing the gender bender myself [made me realize] that we all kind of have a little bit of everything inside of us. . . . Allowing yourself to be open and experience and express different things just really kind of opens your eyes and your thoughts of gender and who you are and people around you." Wes Starr also explained that doing drag helped him to be more open minded about gender: "Being from the South, you're raised a certain way, you're raised with a closed mind, and I didn't really understand why somebody would want to change their gender or change their sex. But doing drag or seeing other people do drag and seeing how comfortable somebody could be in that, in that persona, helped me understand that some people just like to be that way. Some people aren't meant to be a certain gender . . . it's their way to be who they really want to be." In a southern context, positive messages about queer cultures or trans identities are uncommon, and drag provides, in many cases, the only source of information, as opposed to being one of many sources available in other parts of the country.

Trans and nonbinary people face increased obstacles to obtaining health care and are less likely to have health insurance than cisgender people (dickey et al. 2016), especially in the South. The majority of trans and nonbinary kings I spoke with felt that access to health care and the quality of health care they received were directly related to their gender identity. These kings explained that they were denied access to health care due to discrimination based on their gender identities, living in the southeastern United States, and a lack of financial resources. Moreover, Guadalupe-Diaz (2019, 34) predicts that "trans discrimination in health care is likely to get worse before it gets better." Guadalupe-Diaz (2019) points to the fact that the Department of Health and Human Services, under the administration of President Donald Trump, created the Division of Conscience and Religious Freedom, which will allow healthcare workers to deny necessary medical care to queer people on the basis of religious freedom. The inability to procure adequate health care is also compounded by higher rates of uninsured people and higher rates of poverty in the South (Bishaw 2014). Additionally, these "combined struggles of poverty, job insecurity, and homelessness often leave trans people with few options for income," and frequently force them into the underground economy of survival sex (Guadalupe-Diaz 2019, 37) and selling drugs.

Overall, most kings in this study struggled to piece together the resources necessary and the money needed to meet their basic health needs, as well as their transition goals. The kings who desired to physically transition were often unable to do so due to a lack of financial resources. Papi Chulo explained, "I cannot wait for the day that I can get up enough money to have top surgery [a surgical procedure to remove the breasts and construct a more masculine-appearing chest]. Unfortunately, it may not be for years, because forking over ten grand isn't exactly the easiest when you've been bouncing from place to place, staying in your car, being homeless." This was especially problematic for those for whom physical transition is necessary for their psychological well-being. As Matt Mixer puts it, "My decision [to have surgery] is based on how I feel comfortable with my body when I look in the mirror." Therefore, due to financial constraints and lack of sufficient insurance coverage, some of the kings were forced to live uncomfortably, at least in the short term. For some, the amount of money necessary for physical transition seemed like an insurmountable obstacle to happiness.

Even if kings were insured and had financial resources available, most still found it difficult to actually locate services to meet their needs. King Axel explained, "I drive two hours . . . for checkups at Planned Parenthood, because no doctors in my area were really welcoming to trans patients." Planned Parenthood is one of the few medical resources that noninsured or low-income trans and nonbinary people have access to in the South, and it is a resource that is constantly under attack. Planned Parenthood offers education, resources, referrals, and support groups for queer patients, but what many trans people travel for is the ability to access hormone therapy. Most southern states have a couple of clinics, usually located in bigger cities (Atlanta, Savannah, Charleston, Columbia, Birmingham, etc.), while some states, like Mississippi, have only one Planned Parenthood clinic for the entire state. Even when a clinic is available, as King Axel said, most people do not live close by, and must be able to afford to travel in order to receive services.

This is why queer community is so important for locating healthcare resources in the region. Justin Time said, "Living in the South has hindered the process of locating physicians who are trans and nonbinary friendly. The best way to locate these providers would be to ask your local queer community if they know of any, and/or look up places online and call them yourself." These "friendly" physicians are difficult to locate, and often refuse to advertise that they are friendly out of fear of losing other patients. As Rivers Cuomo explained, "There are resources here, but they are limited and operate fairly underground."

Consequently, many kings mentioned the importance of mentoring other trans and nonbinary people. About a third of the kings who wished to physically transition found resources through other trans people or drag kings. Diego Wolf said he was able to locate healthcare resources in Georgia, but clarified, "It does require extensive research; most of this research comes from direct referral within the drag/trans community." Relatedly, Skyler D. Light explained that finding resources "has been incredibly hard, and

I was only able to find them because I am deep in the [queer] community. I often offer my knowledge to trans individuals who do not have the same access to the community that I do, to aid them in their transitions."

Not only must trans and nonbinary people provide education and support for their trans and nonbinary peers; often they must also educate their medical care providers as well. Johnny Walker discussed how he helped educate his therapist about trans issues and how to support trans and nonbinary people: "I have been able to help [the therapists] with understanding transgender individuals more and how they can support us." While it is generally easier to find mental health professionals with experience treating gender issues in other areas of the country, especially in more urban and suburban areas, in the Southeast, and more generally in rural areas, some trans and nonbinary drag kings are forced to use their knowledge of the community to help educate medical professionals. Johnny Walker saw this as activism in order to help his trans and nonbinary community have more resources and more competent healthcare providers in the region.

Interestingly, trans kings were more likely to find adequate health resources than were the kings who identified as nonbinary. This supports research showing that, due to the transnormativity and gatekeeping of medical providers, trans people who wish to physically transition are able to locate adequate health care at a higher rate than those who do not wish to transition (see A. Johnson 2015, 2016, 2019). Medical transition is an important step for some trans people, but "the privileging of this model over others creates a marginalizing effect for gender-non-conforming people who cannot or do not wish to medically transition" (A. Johnson 2016, 466; Rogers 2020). More research is needed to understand fully the obstacles that nonbinary people face in the South.

Concluding Thoughts

Overall, drag is an essential resource in the South for people who do not identify as cisgender and heterosexual. While some other areas of the country, particularly urban areas in the Northeast and the Pacific Northwest, become more accepting and offer more resources for queer people (Transgender Law Center 2020), the Southeast remains a location with limited resources and high levels of prejudice and discrimination against this population. This is likely true of other regions in the United States as well, specifically the Midwest (Mathers 2017; Piontek 2002), which also continues to enforce more conservative political and religious values. Regional studies of drag kinging help to expand our understanding of gender and diversity, and of queer lives in areas of the country where queer visibility is often lacking (Piontek 2002).

Drag can be a resource for understanding gender when other resources are lacking. Drag helped many of the trans and nonbinary kings in this study put their own identity into words and find resources to support that identity; it is an avenue for kings to discover the identities they are forced to hide from the outside world. While some nonbinary kings did discuss "gender identity shifts" (Shapiro 2007), the majority of kings explained that they have always been trans or nonbinary, but they *discovered* this identity through drag. Due to homophobia, transphobia, and the continued emphasis on stereotypical gender norms in the Southeast, gender and sexual identities must be figured out in a largely unaccommodating atmosphere. While drag is a resource for queer people in the South, it should not be the only one.

4
Controversies in the Drag King Community

Justin Case started performing drag about fourteen years ago, when he was twenty-one years old. During his time on the drag scene, he witnessed many of the internal controversies and inequalities where he lived and performed in South Carolina. As he put it, within the drag community "we have our own discrimination that happens." Justin explained, "Drag queens will definitely have their own attitudes about drag kings and what they do. Especially in the South, I found drag queens didn't take drag kings kind of seriously unless you really kind of broke the mold and stood out there. They just kind of saw the drag kings as, 'Oh, those kids are just kind of playing.'" At the same time, he said a lot of the kings felt that the queens were "just over the top and old crotchety ladies." Overall, Justin said there was a lot of "animosity between the two groups."

Justin Case believed a lot of this animosity was due to the age differences between kings and queens, since the kings were generally much younger than the queens. But, he said, it was also related to the fact that "drag queens kind of felt an ownership of the space, like 'This is my dressing room table,' and 'I need all of this space.'" Due to the animosity, kings and queens rarely performed together in South Carolina when Justin was performing there. Justin felt that if kings and queens performed together more, it might have eased the tension and helped the kings succeed. Another South Carolina king, Jinx, agreed that queens were not open to mentoring kings when he started doing drag in the mid-2000s. He said, "Queens weren't really interested in us even being around, so nobody was, like, mentoring." The lack of mentorship also left many kings struggling to learn the art, get booked for shows, and receive fair pay for performing. This animosity between queens and kings likely also mirrors the animosity between queer men and women more generally.

Assuming that "everyone with the same stigma is going to be a so-called sympathetic other" is a faulty assumption (Orne 2013, 248). Queer communities and spaces are not "uniformly safe or welcoming" to all queer people (Orne 2013, 248). As Orne explains, "Since there is so much diversity of identity and expression within queer communities, queer people can feel in the line of fire in these places too. . . . No community is monolithic" (Orne 2013, 248). Studies have demonstrated that the queer community has been less than fully accepting of certain groups, especially trans and bisexual people (Curry 2014; Roberts, Horne, and Hoyt 2015). While the positive benefits of drag far outweigh the negatives, it is still important to explore some of the controversies within this community and how these relate to and perpetuate inequalities within and outside of drag. My hope is that the drag community can be self-reflexive and adjust to become an even more accepting and open community for queers in the South who need these spaces and communities to be themselves without fear of judgment.

From interviews with sixty drag kings between 2013 and 2019, I found that there are four major controversies within the drag king community in the South. The first controversy concerns who is a drag king and how drag kings should perform. This controversy overlaps with the others, but I focus on the divisions between experienced and less experienced kings, which is often, but not always, related to the age of the kings. What kings wear and how they perform can cause a lot of tension between newer, usually younger kings and more experienced, usually older kings.

The second controversy I explore is between cis, usually lesbian, women who perform as kings, and trans men who perform as kings. Often, older kings and cis women kings feel that trans men should no longer perform as drag kings after they initiate any type of physical transition, such as taking hormones or undergoing gender affirmation surgeries. Trans kings are often accused of cheating, and divisions have emerged within the queer community due to this controversy. There is a similar generational controversy within drag queening between cis and trans queens.

The third controversy involves the continued division between drag kings and drag queens. Queens often feel a sense of entitlement to drag, which is related to their masculine power outside of drag and queens' longer history with this type of performance. Although kings perform masculinity on stage, they are usually assumed to be female-bodied underneath their attire by audiences and bar owners, and therefore not entitled to male privilege. Queens, who are assumed to be male-bodied, usually have more power within drag. This is related to the performers' claims to the privileges attached to male bodies in our society. Additionally, because there are very few lesbian bars left in the southeastern United States (and the United States more generally), it is largely cis gay men who own the remaining queer bars and control who gets to perform, which nights they perform, and how much they get paid. Furthermore, some queens feel that the kings do not put in as much work as queens do for their performances, or that kings are simply not as entertaining as queens, and they make their feelings known.

The fourth controversy is one that I witnessed but was not discussed by the drag kings: the way misogyny and homophobia were used to perform masculinities in drag. While drag kinging is often viewed as a critique of masculinity, in a lot of ways in the South it has become a celebration of some of the most toxic components of masculinity. Because of this, drag may be inadvertently propping up toxic versions of masculinities and thereby undoing the potential revolutionary power of drag king performances.

What Not to Wear

The division between theatrical kings and those "flaunting their own masculinity rather than some theatrical imitation of maleness" is not new (Halberstam 1998). Nevertheless, this division continues to lead to hostilities within the drag king community. The kings in this study were largely divided by generation on their ideas of how drag kings should dress and perform. Older kings who paved the way for drag kings in the United States in the 1990s and early 2000s felt strongly about the need for the "theatrical imitation of maleness" in drag kinging. On the other hand, many of the younger, less experienced kings used drag as a way to practice masculinities and learn how they wanted to present in their everyday lives.

Many of the younger kings dressed in "street clothes," or everyday men's clothing (e.g., cargo shorts, jeans, T-shirts, button-up shirts with a tie), forgoing the elaborate costuming of drag queens and older, more experienced drag kings. While some of this was by choice, other circumstances, such as costs, also prohibited some kings from being more theatrical and putting more time and effort into their costumes. Most of the kings I talked to are now thirty years old or older (only thirteen of the kings were under thirty as of the writing of this book), and they talked about younger, less experienced kings as a problem in their interviews. Only a few kings in this study admitted to wearing street clothes themselves in their performances, though from my experiences watching drag in South Carolina and around the southeastern United States and my field notes from 2013, the majority of kings did perform in street clothes.

Wes Starr discussed this issue some. He said, "Dress is where it becomes very difficult because I do dress . . . like a guy on the streets so it makes it really hard." As a "butch girl" on the streets, he said it was hard to change his appearance on stage, since he already wears "khaki shorts, polos, button-up shirts, and ties." For Wes, this made it "really hard to not wear your street clothes on the stage, which is kind of frowned upon, but it's almost impossible to get around." He explained that kings who were more feminine in everyday life—those "who weren't butch"—"just had that luxury

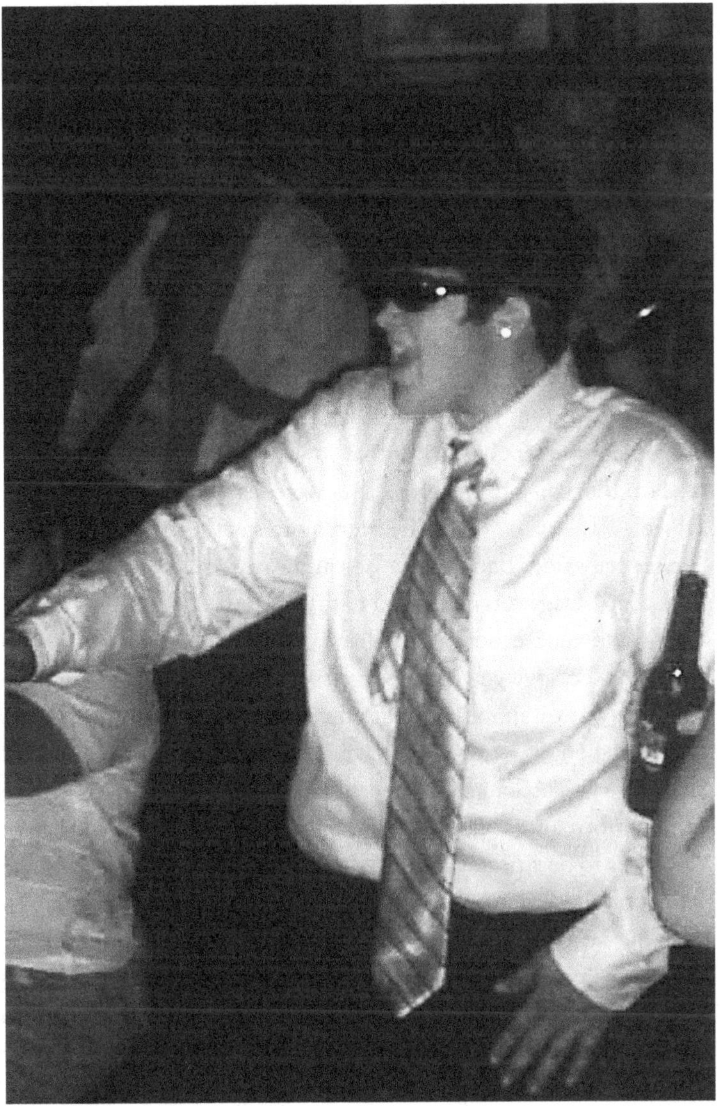

Drag king Wes Starr serenades the audience in a pink shirt and tie.

of different wardrobes" on stage. Ivan Eatner also said, "I dress like I normally do every day basically. Some people say I'm cheating because I'm dressing like I normally do."

Roscoe said that where he performed "it seems like a lot of the younger performers that come into it didn't really put that much effort into it." Roscoe attributed this to the desire of the younger kings to use drag for "the gender expression of it. . . . It's been a way for a lot of younger performers to find their gender identity." Roscoe explained that for at least the last decade he has been performing in Georgia, and that "the over-the-top, over-expression of gender illusion just hasn't been so prevalent here." For him, this was evidence that the art form had declined, which he said was even more apparent in the fact that younger kings didn't even bother to learn the words to the songs they were performing anymore. For Roscoe, "That was very disheartening to say the least."

Roscoe said, "Back in the '90s and early 2000s, if you wanted to get into drag, you really had to prove yourself. You kind of had to find a mentor, or somebody that would backdoor you in and give you a chance, give you a shot at getting out and showing what you got." He was disappointed that now drag competitions and shows let anyone enter: "You don't have to be good." Roscoe explained that there was no longer an expectation that drag kings would make their performances really entertaining. Roscoe felt you had to have resources to be a performer; passion wasn't enough. He said that a lot of younger kings were "not going to have the resources, financially, to keep up with the production costs. There's an old saying, 'Drag ain't cheap, and cheap drag ain't good.' That's very true."

Roscoe said that younger, less experienced kings he tried to mentor "wanted to go shop for fresh little hip-hop kinds of clothes and some kicks and do some little pop songs." He told them they could do that if they wanted, but it would not be entertaining. He said, "You got to bring more than that." Roscoe continued, "You can't go to K-Mart . . . buy shit off the clearance rack, put on an eyeliner moustache, and expect that the crowd is going eat that up and accept you and enjoy it and appreciate it as an illusion, because it's not much work in the illusion."

Patrick Jacquard agreed with Roscoe: "To me, there's different levels of what a drag king does." A good drag performer must go all the way with "facial hair, the clothes, the taping down, all that stuff that's required, all of that. . . . It has to be perfect." He compared top-notch kings that go all out to kings who "just put on basically anything and just go out and just dance there. They don't even wear any facial hair, or they just might mark it on with a marker." This was not the only thing that bothered Patrick about drag today. He was also concerned with performers who did not even attempt gender illusion. He said that some kings were more into costuming but didn't really "transition that much." While he acknowledged that "different people express themselves in different ways in drag," he didn't seem pleased with this. Patrick went on: "It's just like now, we got drag queens that are bearded, which I think is absolutely hideous to me. I don't even understand that. For me, that's like drag king performance with no beard. To me, that's just like cabaret but they do it and people enjoy it, so whatever, whatever excites your audience, then go for it."

When I asked Patrick if he tried to mentor younger, less experienced kings in the art of drag, he said, "Yes, but a lot of them just don't listen." He said they could easily figure things out with YouTube tutorials or asking more experienced kings, but he felt they were just too lazy or hard-headed to listen. Like Roscoe, Patrick believed that younger kings failed to entertain the audience, which, according to these older kings, could also be why drag kinging has not received the same notoriety as drag queening. Patrick expanded: "I think it's like, the kings that are coming out now, especially the younger ones . . . they don't want to do the costume, or they can't afford it, so they think a pair of tennis shoes, blue jeans, and a tie and a shirt is good enough." The problem for Patrick was that this lack of effort affects all drag kings: "I don't think that a lot of the kings honestly offer that [much] entertainment. It's hard to find a king that can hold an audience's attention like a queen. . . . That is very, very difficult to do." While Patrick said he wasn't sure if drag kinging is "dying off," he did say that he knew from audience members that they didn't find most kings entertaining, and that most audience members "want to see the drag queens." This issue was of major concern to Patrick, who brought it up multiple times throughout our interviews. He believed drag kinging could be just as good as drag queening; the problem was that "kings just don't try hard enough."

Justin Case explained that the quality of drag kinging often depended on location, in addition to age and experience. He compared his experiences with drag kinging in Atlanta with those in South Carolina: "In Atlanta, I would say that the bar was kind of set higher, as far as the quality of the drag, the quality of the performances, and costumes of the performers. People were a lot more serious about their art than some of the younger inexperienced kings that were in South Carolina. Because South Carolina, the average age of your drag king was like twenty, twenty-one, twenty-two, as opposed to in Atlanta [where] it was closer to like, twenty-five or thirty." Like Justin Case, Oliver Clothesoff was concerned about drag as a failing art form. Oliver explained, "Something that's important to me, that I always like to voice about drag and drag kings specifically, is that drag is an art. And I feel like drag kings should put as much effort into their art as drag queens do." For Oliver this meant "taking time to tape down, making sure your hair doesn't look the same in every number, switching your jeans after every song, not going on in what you came off the street with." Oliver said, "Drag kings here have just become a joke almost, and it's really because people stop trying, and I mean you just have to respect what you do. And that's really big to me is just respecting the art of drag."

Frustration over how kings dress and perform drag directly relates to the second controversy—over whether or not trans men should continue to perform as drag kings. While not mutually exclusive, the division between those who see drag as primarily art and entertainment, and those who view it as a more practical way to explore everyday masculinities, leads to conflicts between some kings. One issue that especially concerned older drag kings was whether the gender illusion had to be in contrast to a person's assumed biological sex.

Drag in Transition

For most trans masculine interviewees, drag proved to be a useful tool for gender transition. However, a few of the trans kings mentioned some ways that drag might interfere with gender transition. The main issue was that some trans men continued to be viewed as being "in drag," rather than seen *as men*, even after transition. Because most people continue to understand drag to be a performance of a gender that does *not* align with a person's biological sex, conflict often surfaced between cis kings and trans kings.

Montana explained how drag both helped and hindered his gender transition; drag helped him "take the steps medically" to transition, yet simultaneously he thought it impeded people seeing him as a man. Montana continued, "People still see us as kings or male illusionists and that's insulting. They don't take [my transition] seriously. I'm not a male illusionist. I am male." Similarly, Ryder Cox explained that while drag helped him "ease people into seeing me the way I see myself," he found that often he and other trans men were excluded from drag after they began their gender transitions. According to Ryder, this exclusion was based on the belief that trans men were "no longer giving full illusions or [were] no longer a drag king." This loss of community was extremely hurtful and devastating for some trans kings, especially because drag is such an important resource for many trans kings during transition. Skyler D. Light said there is a "weird stigma that if you're trans you must stop doing drag, or you're not allowed to do it anymore, which is sometimes hard to fight against. But, drag is what saved my life and I love it. Why would I turn my back on it at my happiest?"

D-Luv Saviyon also struggled with being pushed out of the community and being seen differently after his transition began. D-Luv explained that after transition, "you start to kind of feel in between, stuck in between, because you start to present more as a male in some cases. . . . It's harder because for a lot of the kings you have to struggle and go back and forth with, because they think you no longer belong. It's almost like you're in a way being exiled from what you've done for years. You can't really compete." D-Luv was hopeful that things were getting better and that in a few years the exclusion of trans kings would not be an issue. Although he still performs and sees evidence that things are getting better, he said "it hurts my feelings a lot. . . . It hurts my feelings because a lot of the kings feel like they don't have the capacity to beat a trans man that happens to do drag . . . and that's not the case, and I've seen it, and I've experienced it. I've been beaten by [cis] kings." Overall, D-Luv said that excluding trans kings from performing drag was "just another reason for separation that should not exist."

Despite his feelings that this separation was unnecessary, D-Luv started to refer to himself as a "male entertainer" rather than a drag king. While he continues to perform in drag shows, and continues to fight for trans inclusion, he said he feels more comfortable calling himself a male entertainer "because I'm not fully a king anymore." In fact, D-Luv explained that he "waited a long time before transitioning because of drag." He started to transition slowly, opting for testosterone pills rather than shots, and was just scheduling his top surgery when we talked for the second time in 2019. Overall, D-Luv said drag made his transition "a very hurtful process . . . because I didn't want to be ousted, because at the time that I started transitioning, it was not as well-received." Since he still had "some major pageants" he wanted to win as a drag king and wanted to remain involved in drag, D-Luv kept his transition quiet for years. Eventually, he said he came to a "fork in the road" and asked himself, "Am I going to try to be deceptive, or am I just going to go ahead and basically advocate for this, and so I just came out about it."

D-Luv, like other trans kings in this study, knew that coming out as trans could lead to trouble in the drag community and that they were likely to face transphobia and cisnormativity within the drag and queer community. D-Luv explained that some people in the queer community "feel [trans men] are not real men and freely speak their opinions." Skyler D. Light agreed that "not everyone in the community is as educated as you would think about gender identities, and sometimes that can lead to people saying hurtful slurs or transphobic things." Abs Hart, a thirty-two-year-old transgender male in Arkansas, discussed how gay men and drag queens often did not understand his relationship with his partner, who also identifies as a man. Abs said, "Many people do not understand the difference between gender identity and sexuality. They're fine with me being a trans man until I try to explain that I'm attracted to men. I also get a lot of 'Wow, I thought you were a real boy!' Well . . . I am." These incidents make it evident that the normative expectations of gender and sexuality in the southern United States do not disappear merely because someone is part of the queer community. Trans and nonbinary people continued to face prejudice and discrimination, even from other gender and sexual minorities.

Some of the cisgender drag kings in this study displayed this cisnormativity and transphobia in their discussions of trans people. For instance, in 2013 when I first spoke with Tex, he shared some of his thoughts about trans people. Tex explained that he felt that many trans people "don't really check out what they have to go through and what's going to be expected" of them after transition. Tex said once trans men begin to "pass as men," they will then be "expected to be able to do what a man does." In his opinion, trans men "are expected to be as strong as a man, and if you were born female, you'll never get there." He went on to share some other transphobic ideas that he said he tries to share with younger drag performers considering gender transition. For example, Tex was concerned about trans people's ability to have sex after transition, such as trans women losing "the ability to climax" and trans men not being able to "get up . . . unless you get a pump put on it." Overall, Tex felt that many trans people "don't get all their ducks in a row before they start [the gender transition process]." He also worried about the consequences of transitioning, and then "all of a sudden you become a woman again." As Tex's comments demonstrate, despite being part of the drag community for over fifty years, he very much believed that gender was biological and essential, and that being trans meant a specific type of transition for everyone. Additionally, many of his beliefs were rooted in ideas that research has shown to be false, such as the fact that a lot of trans people wish to reverse their transitions or that being trans is a phase.

When I spoke with Tex again in 2019, he seemed to realize that he should not express such negative positions openly, but he was still concerned about trans people, especially within the drag community. Tex said that he did not think it was fair for "males" to be able to compete in drag king contests. He discussed how "North Carolina has now added . . . female-to-male and male-to-female categories in their contests; there cannot be a male participant in the king category." He said this is preferable and provided evidence from a show he saw in South Carolina where a "male" beat four cis women drag kings.

Like Tex, Carson Scott did not feel it was "fair" for trans men to perform as drag kings. Carson explained, "I think drag is drag . . . it's an illusion. . . . The reason I wanted to be in the Unlimited system was because Unlimited is all natural, like you can't be on testosterone . . . you can't have your chest done, you have to be all natural. When you take your clothes off, you're a girl . . . or you're a guy if you're a drag queen." For Carson, the illusion was paramount to drag, which to him meant it was "not fair . . . for someone to be doing drag who has had the surgeries, because then you're not an illusion anymore, and that's what drag is, an illusion." Carson said that trans people performing drag after they have physically altered their bodies makes him "upset." He explained, "If I was to go into a bar and do a performance and here's a drag king who's had his chest done and here I've got to tape mine . . . that just bothers me."

One trans drag king seemed to concur with Carson, at least to some degree. Ryder Cox identified as a trans male, or a man, but had not started to physically alter his body when we spoke last in 2017. He said that he was in therapy and beginning to transition but had not started testosterone or had any surgeries yet. Ryder said, "I am a male. . . . I only wear guy clothing. I bind every day. . . . The only time that I give my legal name and sex is in situations where I have to, like at the hospital or if I get pulled over or something like that." Despite the fact that Ryder identified as a man, he felt that after he started altering his body he would probably stop performing as a drag king. He explained, "I do contemplate sometimes after my surgery if I will continue to do drag. Because I don't know that I would still consider myself a drag king, if that makes any sense. Because at that point, I feel like if I were gonna do drag I'd have to dress as a female."

While Ryder understood that men could technically still perform as drag kings, he felt that it just was not "the same." He said after performing as a drag king for almost eight years, he has always been impersonating a man, so after transition, when he finally feels that he is fully a man he is concerned that drag will no longer make sense. Ryder expanded: "So now, I'm getting to the point where I'm questioning with myself if I should continue as a king once I go through this transformation. . . . I feel like I'm just myself on stage. I'm not, I'm no longer trying to portray someone else." Ryder said he didn't know of many trans kings who had continued to perform after they started physically transitioning. For Ryder, trans men performing as kings after physically altering their bodies "almost felt like an advantage especially in a competition. I don't feel like if you have completely transformed, that you should be able to be in a drag king competition, because you're no longer a female to male king. You're a male." While Ryder felt that he would have to stop performing after he started hormones and had top surgery, he did say that "there's so much more into that that I would need to learn about both sides to make a definite decision on what I believe."

Trey Alize discussed at length his thought process and coming to terms with trans people performing drag. He said that trans people performing drag has "been a big debate." To Trey, it seemed to come on the scene all at once, when "a lot of our kings . . . had been a part of the scene for a long time, then started coming out as trans." Trey admitted that he was worried at first:

> My brain at first was in the thought process that what I do is a male illusion. I am impersonating a male and it takes—I have to do a lot of work. I'm a tomboy still, but I still have really

> girly features, especially my face and what not. . . . When the trans community first started coming around . . . I talked very openly with my trans community here because you're not seeing it with a disadvantage, you're not having to work like I am. You're growing that facial hair; you're taking the hormones that are putting your body in a different shape than mine. Some of you no longer have a chest or even worry about binding. . . . To me it felt for a long time a disadvantage, and why would you want to call yourself a drag king or a male illusionist when you're not illusioning? You are a man; there is no illusion there.

Eventually Trey said he realized that even though trans kings may no longer be illusionists or impersonators, they were still drag kings "because they are capitalizing their own self, or their own character on stage. That put something in perspective for me." Trey said he still has issues when trans drag kings call themselves illusionists, because calling trans men illusionists to him feels like "saying you're not a man." He said he now sees that a lot of trans drag kings "go above and beyond because they are trying so hard to still have their place. The makeup they're doing, the costumes they're doing, all of that is still drag, still for entertainers. It's a very hyperized character of a male that they're putting on stage." So, while Trey acknowledged that he "was also part of the resistance when it first happened," he now felt he was more accepting and hoped that the drag scene in Tennessee would follow suit. He said, "Nashville's still, I think, a few years behind on that perspective and that kind of thinking and how that you can come on stage, all forms of drag and it's still all drag, because it's an art form."

For Trey, ostracizing trans kings was really no longer an option, especially in his local community, where the majority of kings had started transitioning. Trey guessed that about "90 percent of our king community is trans." He said locally, only himself and a couple other drag kings he knew were not currently transitioning. He said that the wave of trans kings in Nashville created a community, a family, for trans people:

> They were all getting up on stage together, they were all sharing their stories, they were in path together, so it became this massive community . . . [where trans people could] talk through that "I don't feel comfortable in my own skin. I feel, maybe, I was born with the wrong parts." Those conversations, I think, especially happened backstage with us. We were a big family, you see. We all know each other, we see each other every week or even beyond that if we're doing other shows, or pageants, and different things that happen around town, because we are in Nashville. . . . I think that's what, actually, is the big difference with the community and a family here. The trans kings finding a comfortable place and somewhere they felt okay to be themselves and they felt at home. I think that's why it's become such a dominating thing in our drag community to have trans kings on stage and be predominantly with them. . . . A place to escape. A place to feel at home in Nashville and in their own setting.

Trey explained that he now felt proud to be a part of a drag community that was so trans inclusive.

Diego Wolf said that while he had not personally experienced transphobia in drag, he understood that it was a huge issue "that's everywhere from the basic level to the high level." Diego used *RuPaul's Drag Race* as an example, saying that even at this highest level of televised drag competitions you would find "some of the biggest critics of trans performers there is." He went on to say that, on one hand, "You do get also, not just people in the drag community, that take this viewpoint of, if you're transgender, you have either an unfair advantage because you're transitioning . . . or because you're not really doing drag anymore, because you no longer . . . have to utilize that type of makeup or facial hair technique to create the illusion of a beard because you grow it now." On the other hand, Diego also explained that there is "a group of people out there that are transgender that criticize drag as a mockery of transgender." He said that he does not agree with this sentiment at all. Diego described how this group of trans people boycott an annual drag show he is a part of in Georgia. He said they "pretty much want to equate a drag show to the old historical minstrel shows, and they look at it as people making fun of the trans lifestyle. To those transgender people I'd say, 'No, you have it all wrong, because as a transgender person drag allows me to become who I am. It was the very first door that opened for me in my transition.'" Overall, Diego said, "It's really weird to be a trans person who performs in drag and who receives incidents of hate and judgment from other trans people who absolutely have no idea what they're talking about, to be honest."

Kings versus Queens

While some of the kings had good relationships with queens, many felt that the relationships between kings and queens were tense due to power inequalities in the drag scene. While in drag, kings claim masculinity. Nevertheless, the queens are presumed to have male bodies, and the differential power that confers outside of drag usually translates into more power within the drag scene. Much of the inequality between drag kings and queens is also linked to the fact that most queer bars today are owned and run by cis gay men, not cis lesbian women or trans people. While the number of queer bars has declined in general, "lesbian bars have probably always been more vulnerable than their men's counterparts" (Wilson 2020). Money is a major reason that lesbian bars have disappeared, as "income inequality has historically meant less disposable income for women" (Wilson 2020). Overall, women make less money than men, are less able to support women-owned businesses, and have a more difficult time accessing capital to open businesses. As Wong (2019) explains, "The lesbian bar, often owned and run by women, is slowly leaving the nightlife scene in cities across the country." In fact, "from a historic perspective, there were more lesbian bars in the 1930s than there are today" (Wong 2019). For a specific example, in New York City in 2019 there were only three remaining lesbian bars, compared to the forty-plus gay bars (Wong 2019).[12]

12. For more on the decline in the lesbian bar scene, check out the podcast *Unladylike*, episode 35: "How to Find a Lesbian Bar."

The disappearance of lesbian space is directly related to the decline in the drag king scene in the United States and around the world (Drysdale 2019). With only a couple of women-owned lesbian bars remaining in the South, drag kings' schedules and pay are largely controlled by cis gay men and drag queens today. The fact that gay men and drag queens are gatekeepers to drag culture has resulted in kings receiving less space and time within the drag scene.

Roscoe McCoy explained some of the problems with queens being the gatekeepers to drag. When he moved to a new city in Georgia, he said, "I had to re-establish myself over here, because everything here was run by the same clique of drag queens, and they didn't give a damn who you were or where you had performed or anything like that." Roscoe went on, "The queens run the scene, so if you don't get in with queens, you don't get stage time. You don't get a shot." According to Roscoe, "If you didn't kiss ass for certain queens, you weren't in the clique, you couldn't get into a bar, and you couldn't get booked." However, Roscoe said, "My personal experience here has been that the queens that control that flow are not the ones that I want to owe favors to."

Ayden said he wished there were "more unifications between drag kings and drag queens." Ayden thought that a lot of the division between the kings and queens was related to a divide between "the lesbian world and the gay man world," worlds he believed "cannot mix because of whatever judgments or whatever preconceptions they have about either group." He went on to say that as in the world outside of drag, rarely do gay men and lesbian women mix: "You've got your gay men, you've got your gay bars, and you've got lesbian bars, and you've got your lesbian night at the gay bar." Ayden lamented that drag was supposed to offer "a place where everybody can laugh at themselves . . . be carefree for a bit," but he said that the "tension between those two groups is not very attractive and can be felt within the audience as well." Ideally, Ayden wished that everyone could just "get along." He hoped that the queer community could overcome its divisions because "we are more dynamic when we all come together and everybody knows that, that's how it is in every single group, nation, tribe, whatever. I think it would be more powerful if we came together more."

Finally, Ryder Cox, who was among the first kings on the scene in South Carolina, said that "some of the queens maybe felt like their toes were being stepped on." Like some other kings I spoke to, Ryder believed that queens felt animosity toward kings because they believed kings did not, or did not have to, put in as much effort as queens to perform. He said, "Once [queens] realized that we do put work into it and we do have to learn all our lyrics just like they do, pick outfits, and put on an actual performance and not just stand on stage and, you know, lip-synch," the queens started to respect kings more.

Newer kings, those who started performing in the 2010s, did not discuss the controversy between kings and queens as much as the older kings. In fact, many of the newer kings were very close to queens, and some performed with queens regularly. While further research is needed, hopefully this is some evidence that drag queens have begun to respect kings more and that they are working together to improve the drag scene rather than fighting over whom the space and time belong to. Nevertheless, as lesbian bars continue to disappear and few queer and inclusive spaces pop up to take their place, cis gay men and drag queens will continue to have more power in the drag scene in the United States. Until men, women, and trans people are treated equally in society at large, inequality will likely continue in the drag scene as well. Unfortunately, some of the drag king performances I have witnessed in the South are not doing much to promote a move to a more equitable distribution of power between men, women, and trans people in society.

Misogyny and Homophobia in Drag

While drag provides a lot for the queer community, such as space to be free and have fun, a safe place to play with gender, and resources for understanding gender and sexual identities, drag is not always progressive and positive. Sometimes the toxic elements of gender are celebrated in drag rather than parodied or critiqued. Some kings fell into the trap of reinforcing toxic versions of masculinities rather than calling them out as problematic. While these could be viewed by an outside observer as harsh commentaries on toxic masculinities, the performers made clear that this was not their intention. In these cases, drag kings can normalize misogyny, homophobia, and violence as acceptable, or even celebrated, parts of masculinity.

I vividly remember the most extreme example of this I witnessed at a drag show in Columbia, South Carolina, around the year 2009, before I began this research. I attended a drag king show at the only bar exclusively dedicated to drag performances, PT's Cabaret. The drag king set up the stage with a couch and had a cis woman performing with him. The song the king performed to was "I Want to Fuck You Like an Animal" by Nine Inch Nails. Some of the lyrics are "You let me violate you; You let me desecrate you; You let me penetrate you; You let me complicate you. . . . I want to fuck you like an animal; I want to feel you from the inside; I want to fuck you like an animal; My whole existence is flawed; You get me closer to God." As this song played, the king acted out a rape scene on the couch with the woman. It was a very disturbing and graphic display of an extremely violent act. No one in the audience seemed to be bothered by this performance. It was a popular song, and violence and rape were accepted by the audience and the performers as a "normal" part of performing masculinity.

During the first part of this study in 2013, when I attended a number of drag shows around South Carolina, I witnessed another drag king minimize the seriousness of rape as part of his drag act. It was a Saturday night show at a lesbian bar, and Ayden was the king MC for the night. He begins the show dressed as and playing the role of a drunken Jack Sparrow (the main character in *Pirates of the Caribbean*). Ayden has two boxes with him that he explains are going to be used to play games with the audience members. He starts by making jokes about how he loves boxes and that he is a box enthusiast, making gestures to clarify that the boxes are an innuendo for vaginas. Then, in his best pirate's voice he talks about "raping and pillaging" his way through the bar. Later in the show, Ayden comes on stage holding a golden dildo with Obama's head as the tip and says he can't wait to take Obama home with him.

In addition to these problematic performances of violence and toxic masculinity, the incorporation of misogyny and homophobia, along with the lack of challenge to toxic elements of masculinity, was evident in some of the kings' drag names, attire, and song choices. Drag names like Ivan Eatner (pronounced "I've been eating her"), Liquor Down (pronounced "Lick her down"), and Oliver Clothesoff (pronounced "All of her clothes off") are clearly sexual in nature. Each implies heterosexuality; the king being a "real" man, he must be sexually involved with a woman ("her"). Another way to suggest they are men is through references in their stage names and performances to having a penis, such as Ryder Cox and Shawn Lance Hardwood. This is part of the act, an exaggeration of masculinities for performance, but the kings often adopt these personas, and this carries over outside of the act and influences how they think of what of it means to be a man.

As an illustration of the importance of heterosexuality to performing manhood, Carson Scott, who labeled his gender and sexual identity as "just me," explained that he liked performing with drag queens because they were more entertaining, and he found performing difficult when it was a night for drag kings only: "I do a lot of duets with drag queens and so that was just weird having the just boys thing. It was nice to have a female, I mean a drag queen, in the mix. It kinda gives it more of a spice, you know what I'm saying, because most drag queens are funny . . . and it's kinda hard for another boy to compliment another boy. . . . Most drag queens who work the mic are gonna be like, 'The lovely, sexy Carson Scott,' you know, it's kinda hard for another boy to be like 'sexy Carson.' It doesn't sound the same." Although Carson said if he had to pick a sexuality label other than "just me," it would be gay, he still felt that he needed a drag queen to compliment him on the stage. This also demonstrates how masculinities are always expected to be heterosexual, because another "boy" complimenting him would be "hard."

Most of the kings I observed performing dressed in stereotypical men's clothing and performed songs about their desire to be with women in heteronormative sexual activities. For example, one performer lip-synched Ginuwine's song "In Those Jeans," with the lyrics "Looking good, plenty tight, tell me is there any more room for me in those jeans? Really thick like I like it; Tell me is there any more room for me in those jeans?" Another king chose the song "Baby Let Me Take You Home" by the Animals ("Baby let me take you home; I'll love you all my life; You can bet I'll treat you right; If you'll just let me take you home"). While he was performing, a drag queen jumped on stage and pretended to have a sexual encounter with him.

During my observations for this book, as well as in my own personal experience with drag in the southeastern United States, I never witnessed a drag king performance that overtly challenged sexism, racism, or homophobia the way that previous research has shown takes place in other areas of the country. In a previous article (Baker and Kelly 2016), I argued that this is evidence of the inability or unwillingness of drag kings in the Southeast to use drag kinging as a tool for social change. Rather than doing drag for political reasons, for the most part southern drag kings perform drag to escape the reality that female and trans masculinities are devalued in the South. Challenging blatant sexism, racism, or homophobia would transform their performances into a political act and seemingly defeat the purpose of escape. The kings' names, song choices, and performances can be seen in contrast, and often contradiction, to overtly political statements for social change made by kings in other areas of the country.

Concluding Thoughts

Performing drag is fun and even helpful for many kings, but like most things, there are pros and cons. The major problems within the drag king community revolve around four controversies: (1) who is a drag king and how should they perform; (2) whether trans men can still perform drag; (3) animosity between drag kings and drag queens; and (4) the misogyny and homophobia perpetuated by drag in the South. Boundaries are what make groups possible, and like all groups, the drag community continues to struggle with where to draw those lines. Should only certain people perform as drag kings? Is there a "right" way to perform drag? Further, what does it mean to be exclusive in a community largely made up of queer people who have been excluded from so many other areas of their lives?

While these controversies continue in the drag community today, there is evidence that some of these issues have started to be resolved, at least in certain areas across the South. Queens seem more accepting of kings than they used to be. Most kings today accept and embrace trans people and believe that trans people should be able to continue to perform drag. Although I have not been to many drag king–specific shows since my observations in 2013, I have seen kings and queens performing together often. Also, I have not witnessed blatant violence, misogyny, or homophobia performed by a drag king recently. Nevertheless, the questions of who should be called a king and how they should perform persist, and the names, songs, and performances kings choose often implicitly reinforce or normalize sexism, homophobia, and heteronormativity in the South.

Conclusion

Overall, the goal of this book is to provide a missing piece of queer history, a look at drag king culture in the southern United States. Through my time performing as Macon Love, my research and observations for this book, and the rich stories of drag kings across the region, it is clear that drag has many sociological implications for drag kings and queer people more generally. Too much sociological work to date has been decontextualized and leaves unexamined the importance of geographical location for various experiences, especially the experiences of queer people. This book traces the history of drag and why it continues to be a vital resource in the southern United States. I also assess controversies within the drag community that demonstrate that all communities have things to work on. Equality and acceptance are not things we can arrive at in a country that is structurally unequal and biased. Everyone must continue to strive for equality and acceptance within our own communities, as well as in society at large.

Challenging and Reinforcing the Gender Binary

One reason I began researching drag kings back in 2013 was to try to understand whether drag kinging challenges or reinforces the gender binary, and all of the problems that accompany this binary, such as sexism, homophobia, transphobia, and so on. I found that, as with most cultures, this is more a complex question of both/and, rather than either/or. Drag both challenges and reinforces the gender binary. Nevertheless, with a radical history and a potential for a queer and radical future, drag can be a powerful outlet for change.

Drag kinging started out of a radical desire for cis women to gain some of the power and privileges of cis men through performance. Dating back to the first male impersonators in the United States in the 1860s, dressing and performing masculinity allowed cis women access to spaces they were previously denied. In the early 1900s, male impersonation provided an avenue for masculine women to feel comfortable, especially within the dyke bar scene. Finally, when drag kinging began to surface in the United States in the early 1990s, it was mainly performed by cis lesbian women who felt that gender dynamics in the United States should and could be challenged.

These feminist ideals of challenging male-bodied people's sole access to masculinities, and challenging the larger culture based on a gender binary, did not necessarily translate smoothly into the southeastern United States in the early 1990s. Rather, drag kinging in the South largely began with lesbians seeking a momentary escape from the larger homophobic culture of the region. These women were not necessarily trying to challenge the culture as much as to remove themselves from it for a moment of escape. Further, the different socioeconomic, religious, and political backgrounds of the lesbians who started the drag king scenes in other areas of the United States versus those in the South meant that most southern kings did not identify themselves as feminists early on.

In 2013, none of the kings I interviewed explicitly claimed to be a feminist, and only a few seemed to identify at all with the mission of feminism as a struggle for equality among all genders. In fact, eight of the twenty-seven kings I talked to in 2013 did not know what feminism meant, and only six kings felt that drag was an overtly political act. When I interviewed thirty-eight trans and nonbinary kings in 2017, all but a couple of the kings knew what feminism meant, and twenty-seven (71 percent) of the kings identified themselves as feminists to some degree. Only four years after my initial interviews, the southern kings I spoke with appeared to be more politically involved and ready to challenge the gender binary. Obviously, speaking with only trans and nonbinary kings had some influence on this, but even some of the kings I spoke with in both 2013 and 2017 had learned more about feminism and many now proudly identified themselves with the label.

In 2017, Mike Hunt, a thirty-four-year-old multiracial straight male in Georgia, described feminism as "equality for all. I don't think it's just about empowering women, but instead empowering us all to want equal rights and equal respect." When I asked Mike if he considered himself a feminist, he said, "Hell yeah I'm a feminist! We all should be feminists . . . but then we'd achieve world peace and Miss America wouldn't have anything to tell the judges." Along the same lines, Rivers Cuomo said that a feminist is "an intelligent badass with the capacity to see and celebrate the wonders and joys of both femininity and masculinity and uses both to their greatest advantage." When I asked Rivers if he considered himself a feminist, he said, "Of course. I don't let my vagina keep me from engaging in masculine pursuits, just as I don't allow it to force me into femininity that is inauthentic to myself." Overall, it seems that even in the southeastern United States, drag kings are becoming more political and are starting to use drag as a resource to challenge the gender binary rather than just as an escape from a conservative culture.

Other Significant Implications

This study demonstrates the necessity of drag kinging in the South and the need to support this art form in order to keep this subculture viable. While drag queening has witnessed more mainstream acceptance and encouragement over the last decade through shows like *RuPaul's Drag Race* and public libraries hosting "Drag Queen Story Hours," drag kings remain in the background. Further, the decline in queer bars, especially lesbian bars, around the country has reduced the number of venues for kings to perform. To save drag kinging, I propose a two-pronged approach. First, if drag kings could break into mainstream culture in the way queens have, this would provide many new and exciting venues for kinging. Moreover, this would allow the general public to witness drag kings play with and break down masculinity in a way that is often hidden from view. There could be drag king story hours to challenge gender and binary conceptions of masculinity. Drag kings could be featured on *RuPaul's Drag Race*. Restaurants could hold drag king brunches, and venues that are not specifically queer could host drag king shows.

Second, there must also be a concerted effort to save queer bars—drag bars and lesbian bars in particular—from the threats of sexism, gentrification, and being mainstreamed to the point of disappearance. While drag kings breaking into mainstream culture could be beneficial for kings and society at large, allowing queer spaces to continue to disappear hurts all queer people. Queer people still need places to escape the ongoing oppression of the broader society and culture. Drag is a queer art that needs queer spaces to continue to grow and thrive. While performing for a mainstream audience could be fun, it will likely also limit expression and cause the performances to lose some of the queer qualities of drag. Additionally, it is problematic that, due to sexism, lesbian women, trans people, and other queer people are unable to sustain bars and spaces in the way that cis gay men have been able to. This points to further inequality within this already marginalized community.

Finally, this study demonstrates the need for more resources for queer people in the southern United States surrounding gender and sexuality. Queer Southerners should not have to perform drag to find basic resources, such as where to seek health care and information about trans identities and gender transition. It is not the responsibility of queer people to adapt to society's standards of gender and sexuality, nor should it be the sole responsibility of queer people to provide resources for other queer people. Rather, "the onus is ultimately upon society to expand the possibilities of gender [and sexuality] so that transgender individuals [and all queer people] may lead more livable lives" (Miller and Grollman 2015,

827). Queer scholars and activists must shift focus in order to understand and meet the diverse needs of those most vulnerable among us and to help guarantee everyone's basic human rights. Despite the stereotypes about the southern United States, many queer people continue to reside in this region and identify as southern, and are fighting for progressive change. We need your help. I urge you not to give up on the South, because that means giving up on me, the kings in this study, and all of the other queer people in the region.

How *You* Can Help!

If you want to be a part of progressive change for queer people in the southern United States, you can join, donate, and/or volunteer with a variety of nonprofits in the region striving to make the South more livable for queer people. Here are some of my favorites:

- ALSO Youth—Sarasota, Florida
- Campaign for Southern Equality—Asheville, North Carolina
- Central Alabama Pride—Birmingham, Alabama
- Equality North Carolina—Raleigh, North Carolina
- Equality Virginia—Richmond, Virginia
- Gender Benders—Upstate South Carolina
- Georgia Equality—Atlanta, Georgia
- Harriet Hancock LGBT Center—Columbia, South Carolina
- Northwest Arkansas Equality—Fayetteville, Arkansas
- OUTMemphis—Memphis, Tennessee
- Pridelines—Miami, Florida
- Savannah LGBT Center—Savannah, Georgia
- SisterReach—Memphis, Tennessee
- Southerners on New Ground (SONG)—Atlanta, Georgia
- The Spectrum Center of Hattiesburg—Hattiesburg, Mississippi
- Transcend Charlotte—Charlotte, North Carolina
- TRANScending Barriers—Atlanta, Georgia
- Trans(forming)—Atlanta, Georgia
- We Are Family—Charleston, South Carolina

Additionally, please support your local drag kings and drag queens by going to their shows, tipping the performers, taking your kids to drag story hours, and supporting your local queer bars. The only lesbian bars that I know of in the southeastern United States at the writing of this book are My Sisters Room in Atlanta, Georgia, and Lipstick Lounge in Nashville, Tennessee. Please support them. Together we can all strive for a better, and hopefully queerer, future.

Appendix A

Demographics Table

APPENDIX A. Demographics Table

DRAG NAME OR PSEUDONYM	INTERVIEW ROUND	AGE IN 2020	RACE/ ETHNICITY	LOCATION	GENDER IDENTITY	SEXUALITY	EDUCATION	OCCUPATION
Abs Hart	2	35	White	AR	Transgender male	Gay	Bachelor's	Retail worker
Adonis Black	2	31	Multiracial	NC	Gender fluid	Lesbian	Some College	Credit specialist
Andrew Starr	2	33	Multiracial	FL	FTM	Straight	Master's	Learning and development specialist
Ayden	1	44	White	SC	Female	Lesbian	Bachelor's	Insurance agent
Bastian Sage	2	27	White	TN	Trans man	Straight	High School	Sales associate
Beau Davis	2	27	White	AR	Trans male / stem	Straight	Some College	Kitchen staff
Bo	1	38	White	SC	Woman	Lesbian	Some College	Electrician
Brad Night	2	43	White	SC	Male	Straight	Bachelor's	Corrections officer
Carson Scott	1	44	Native American	SC	No label	No label	Some College	Restaurant cook / construction worker
Chase Down	1	29	White	SC	Girly/stud	Open	Associate's	Gym consultant
Chase Sky	2	28	White	TN	Transgender	Straight	Associate's	Pawnbroker
Colby King	1	33	White	SC	Female	Lesbian	Associate's	Security guard and probation officer
Conner Rush Dupri	1	27	White	SC	Female	Pansexual	High School	Retail worker
Derrick	1	35	White	SC	Female	Gay	High school	Student / insurance representative
Diego Wolf	2, 3	38	White	GA	Transgender man	Straight	Master's	Account manager / sales administrator

D-Luv Saviyon	2, 3	47	African American	TN	Transgender / trans man	Bisexual	Some college	Tech support
Hayden Fury	2	28	White	GA	FTM	Queer	Associate's	Sales associate / drag show director
Hayden Lowe	1, 2	30	White	SC	Nonbinary/ nonconforming	Pansexual	Some college	Guest services associate
Ivan Eatner	1, 2	26	White	SC	Male	Straight	Bachelor's	Gas station attendant / student
Jayden Lee Lowe	1	30	White	SC	Female	Lesbian	Some college	Fast-food worker
Jinx Kelly	1	41	White	SC	Female	Lesbian	High school	Restaurant server
JL Evans-Dickerson	2	37	African American	NC	Female/stem	Pansexual	Associate's	Registered medical assistant
Johnny Walker	2	27	White/ Hispanic	GA	Male	No label	Bachelor's	Social services technician
Jordan Michaels McCord	2	47	White	GA	Female / stud female	Lesbian	Some college	Police officer
Justin Case	1	35	White	SC	Female	Gay	Bachelor's	Army National Guard
Justin Time	2	23	White	SC	Male	Bisexual	Some college	Assistant manager
Kenneth Squires	2	53	White	KY	Female	Lesbian	High school	Housewife
King Axel	2	30	White	SC	Trans man	Queer	Associate's	Firefighter
Levi Vincent	2	30	White	TN	Gender neutral	Lesbian	Some college	Assistant manager
Liquor Down	1	28	Hispanic/ Italian	SC	Woman	Lesbian	Some college	Fast-food worker / student

(*continued*)

APPENDIX A (CONTINUED)

DRAG NAME OR PSEUDONYM	INTERVIEW ROUND	AGE IN 2020	RACE/ ETHNICITY	LOCATION	GENDER IDENTITY	SEXUALITY	EDUCATION	OCCUPATION
LJ Taylor Fury	2	32	White	GA	FTM	Queer	Some college	Delivery driver
Lucas Storm	1	30	White	SC	Transvestite	Lesbian	Some college	Unemployed / drag performer
Matt Mixer	2	31	White	TN	Male	Straight	Bachelor's	Factory supervisor
Mike Hunt	2	34	Multiracial	GA	Male	Straight	Associate's	Customer service
Montana	2	51	White	NC	Male	Straight	Some college	Woodworker / stay-at-home dad
Mr. Brightside	2	22	White	SC	Cis female	Lesbian	GED	Assistant unit director / drag king
Oliver Clothesoff	1	31	White/Jewish	SC	Female	Lesbian	Some college	Hookah Lounge manager
Papi Chulo	2	28	Mexican	TN	Trans male	Pansexual	High school	Fast-food worker
Patrick Jacquard	2, 3	58	White	TN	Female	Lesbian	Associate's	Drag promoter
Phil D. Bern	2	51	African American	KY	Male	Lesbian	Some college	Billing specialist
Prince Dryden	1	35	White	SC	Female	Lesbian	Associate's	Warehouse worker
Rider Oliver Fox	1	25	White	SC	Mentally male	Straight	High school	Jewelry consultant
Rivers Cuomo	2	38	White	SC	Genderqueer	Queer	Master's	Therapist
Romeo	1, 2	35	Multiracial	SC	Female	Lesbian	Some college	Restaurant manager
Roscoe McCoy	2, 3	45	Multiracial	GA	Gender fluid	Omni/ pansexual	Some college	Paramedic and EMS educator
Ryder Cox	1, 2	32	Native American / White	SC	Trans male / man	Straight	Some college	Restaurant server

Shawn Lance Hardwood	1	31	Hispanic	SC	Trans FTM	Straight	Associate's	Certified surgical technologist
Shawn Stud	2	31	White	MS	Androgynous	Bisexual	Master's	Researcher
Shook ByNature	2	35	African American	NC	Androgynous metrostud	Lesbian	Associate's	Private chef and line cook
Sir Cameron Sinklair	1	36	White	SC	Man	Lesbian	GED	Unemployed, on disability
Sir Michael Montgomery	1	57	White	SC	Female	Lesbian	High school	Restaurant manager
Skyler D. Light	2	32	White	GA	Trans male	Queer	Some college	Manager
Soco Dupree	2	36	White	TN	Male	Straight	Some college	Critical response agent
Teddy Michael	2	33	Black	NC	Male	Queer	Some college	Hotel management
Tex	1, 3	66	White	SC	Female	Gay/butch	Some college	Zoning inspector / pro wrestler
Trey Alize	2, 3	35	White	TN	Gender fluid	Lesbian	Bachelor's	Record specialist
Warren Payne	1	33	Pacific Islander / White	SC	Female	Lesbian	Some college	Contracting administrator—Air Force
Wes Starr	1, 2	34	White	SC	Non–gender specific	Lesbian	Bachelor's	Massage therapist
Xavier	1	38	White	SC	Gender neutral	Lesbian	High school	Senior material handler / warehouse worker
Xavier Dupri	1	38	White	SC	Transgender	Straight	Associate's	Entertainer / drag performer

Appendix B

My Queer Methodology

This book is based on data from a combination of interviews, qualitative surveys, observations, and autoethnographic data. The bulk of the analysis is based on interviews and qualitative surveys collected at three different points in time, in 2013 (twenty-seven interviews), 2017 (thirty-eight qualitative surveys), and 2018–2019 (six interviews), with a total of sixty drag kings across the southeastern United States. I situate these interviews and surveys using my recorded observations of five drag shows in South Carolina in 2013, in addition to autoethnographic understandings of drag from my time attending shows and performing in South Carolina and Mississippi between 2008 and 2015. I will discuss each data collect strategy in more detail here.

In 2013, I interviewed twenty-seven drag kings who performed drag in South Carolina. These interviews were conducted in person (twelve) and via phone (fifteen) between April and July 2013. The major goal of the first round of interviews was to understand the content and context of drag king performances in the southeastern United States. I sought to determine whether drag kinging in this region was similar to or different from drag kinging in other areas of the country.

While traveling to conduct interviews with South Carolina drag kings in 2013, I observed five drag shows around the state and took in-depth field notes of these observations. All five observations occurred in June 2013. I attended two king shows at PT's 1109 in

Columbia, one at the L-Word in Cayce, one at the Marlboro Station in Aiken, and one at the Stone Castle in Greenville. These field notes are used to provide context for the interviews and describe the drag king scene in the southeastern United States.

The second round of data collection took place between January and March 2017. During this period, I collected thirty-eight in-depth, qualitative, online surveys from trans and nonbinary drag kings who had performed in the southeastern United States. The goal of these surveys was to understand the relationship between trans and nonbinary identities and drag kinging. All of these surveys were completed independently online. Phone interviews and online surveys both allow respondents increased privacy, which can be beneficial for collecting candid responses from marginalized groups (McDermott and Roen 2012; McInroy 2016).

The third round of interviews occurred in December 2018 and January 2019. I completed six follow-up phone interviews with older drag kings in the southeastern United States in order to gain a better understanding of the history of drag kinging in the South. I invited interviewees from the previous two rounds of data collection who had performed drag for at least ten years in the southeastern United States and were at least thirty years old.

The final method of data collection for this project is autoethnography. This data comes from my time attending drag shows and performing as a drag king in South Carolina and Mississippi between 2008 and 2015. I attended my first drag show in Columbia, South Carolina, in 2008 at PT's Cabaret. This was also where I performed for the first time as a drag king in 2010. Between 2008 and 2015, I attended numerous drag kings shows in both South Carolina and Mississippi and performed as a king approximately five times. I use these experiences attending shows and performing as Macon Love to add further context to my analysis of interviews and surveys with kings across the region.

As a qualitative, feminist sociologist, it is necessary to acknowledge my positionality as a genderqueer lesbian from the Southeast who has performed drag in this region. As a member of the queer community and someone who had performed as a king previously,

I was allowed access to this community that would likely not have been available to other researchers. Personal connections within the drag community helped me to connect with drag kings across the region. Additionally, since I was a member of the queer community, drag kings felt more comfortable sharing their experiences with me than they may have with other academics outside the community. In my recruitment emails for each round of data collection, I self-identified as a drag king who had performed in the region.

The drag king sample for this study was gathered through personal contacts and social media. Having previously performed drag in South Carolina and Mississippi, I had contact with several kings in the southeastern United States. Other interviewees were recruited via social media; specifically, I placed a call for participants on my Facebook page and used the Facebook pages of southern drag bars to find additional participants. I also utilized snowball sampling by asking respondents to recommend other drag kings who may have been interested in this project. Snowball sampling is an effective method for locating hard to reach populations. Many drag kings are part of drag communities that span the region; through snowball sampling I was able to locate drag kings beyond my own network of contacts.

All interviews and surveys were transcribed and coded in MaxQDA—a qualitative software program—using themes that emerged from the data. Kings were asked whether they wished to use their drag names or be provided a pseudonym. Therefore, some of the names in this book reflect kings' chosen drag names, and others are pseudonyms used to protect respondent confidentiality. Keeping the drag names of the kings comfortable with the possibility of being identified is important in order to analyze the names the kings choose.

After listening to and reading the interviews and surveys multiple times, I coded the recurring themes. This coding was conducted with my observations and autoethnographic experience in mind. However, it is important to note that I attempt to explain drag kinging in the South and the various subjects kinging relates to as closely as possible to how the kings saw them. The kings whose stories I share throughout this book are the experts in their own identities and lives. While this may seem obvious, too often in research it is not. While grounded theory played a role in this analysis, queer methods of analysis are much broader and more diverse than grounded theory alone can capture (C. Connell 2018; J. Ward 2018). The data collection strategies for this book are varied, as is the analysis of various aspects of the data.

Acknowledgments

First, thank you to my wife, Sarah, and my daughter, Sutton, for supporting me in everything I do. Thank you to my brother-in-law, Jacob, for his helpful editing skills. Thank you to Mississippi State University, especially my mentor Kimberly Kelly, for the support that allowed me to start this project almost a decade ago. Thank you to all of the anonymous reviewers who helped me improve the quality of this book for publication. Most importantly, thank you to all of the drag kings who have taken time to talk with me over the last decade. Your insights and experiences are the heart of this project, and I am grateful to have been entrusted with your stories.

References

Abelson, Miriam J. 2016. "'You Aren't from Around Here': Race, Masculinity, and Rural Transgender Men." *Gender, Place and Culture* 23, no. 11: 1535–1546.

———. 2019. *Men in Place: Trans Masculinity, Race, and Sexuality in America*. Minnesota: University of Minnesota Press.

American Psychiatric Association. 2013. *Diagnostic and Statistical Manual of Mental Disorders*. 5th ed. Washington, DC: American Psychiatric Association.

Ayoup, Colleen, and Julie Podmore. 2002. "Making Kings." *Journal of Homosexuality* 43, no. 3–4: 51–74.

Bagby, Dyana. 2016. "Charlie Brown, Former Owner Reminisce on Backstreet's Wild Atlanta Ride." *Georgia Voice*. Accessed January 26, 2020. https://thegavoice.com/culture/charlie-brown-former-owner-look-back-backstreets-wild-atlanta-ride/.

Baker, Ashley A., and Kimberly Kelly. 2016. "Live Like a King, Y'all: Gender Negotiation and the Performance of Masculinity among Southern Drag Kings." *Sexualities* 19, no. 1–2: 46–63.

Bariola, Emily, Anthony Lyons, William Leonard, Marian Pitts, Paul Badcock, and Murray Couch. 2015. "Demographic and Psychosocial Factors Associated with Psychological Distress and Resilience among Transgender Individuals." *American Journal of Public Health* 105, no. 10: 2108–2116.

Barton, Bernadette. 2012. *Pray the Gay Away: The Extraordinary Lives of Bible Belt Gays*. New York: New York University Press.

Baunach, Dawn M., Elisabeth O. Burgess, and Courtney S. Muse. 2010. "Southern (Dis)Comfort: Sexual Prejudice and Contact with Gay Men and Lesbians in the South." *Sociological Spectrum* 30, no. 1: 30–64.

Benson, Kristen E. 2013. "Seeking Support: Transgender Client Experiences with Mental Health Services." *Journal of Feminist Family Therapy* 25, no. 1: 17–40.

Bishaw, Alemayehu. 2014. "Changes in Areas with Concentrated Poverty: 2000 to 2010." *American Community Survey Reports*, June 30, 2014. https://www2.census.gov/library/publications/2014/acs/acs-27.pdf.

Bockting, Walter O., Michael H. Miner, Rebecca E. Swinburne Romine, Autumn Hamilton, and Eli Coleman. 2013. "Stigma, Mental Health, and Resilience in an Online Sample of the US Transgender Population." *American Journal of Public Health* 103, no. 5: 943–951.

Bradford, Judith, Sari L. Reisner, Julie A. Honnold, and Jessica Xavier. 2013. "Experiences of Transgender-Related Discrimination and Implications for Health: Results from the Virginia Transgender Health Initiative Study." *American Journal of Public Health* 103, no. 10: 1820–1829.

Brown-Saracino, Japonica. 2018. *How Places Make Us: Novel LBQ Identities in Four Small Cities.* Chicago: University of Chicago Press.

Budge, Stephanie L., Jill L. Adelson, and Kimberly A. S. Howard. 2013. "Anxiety and Depression in Transgender Individuals: The Roles of Transition Status, Loss, Social Support, and Coping." *Journal of Consulting and Clinical Psychology* 81, no. 3: 545–557.

Burton, Gabrielle. 2017. *Kings, Queens, and In-Betweens* [Documentary]. Santa Monica, CA: Five Sisters Productions.

Butler, Judith. 1990. *Gender Trouble: Feminism and the Subversion of Identity.* New York: Routledge.

———. 1993. "Imitation and Gender Insubordination." In *The Lesbian and Gay Studies Reader*, edited by Henry Abelove, Michele Aina Barale, and David M. Halperin, 307–320. New York: Routledge.

Carpenter, Christopher S., and Samuel T. Eppink. 2017. "Does It Get Better? Recent Estimates of Sexual Orientation and Earnings in the United States." *Southern Economic Journal* 84, no. 22: 426–441.

Carter, J. Scott, and Casey A. Borch. 2005. "Assessing the Effects of Urbanism and Regionalism on Gender-Role Attitudes, 1974–1998." *Sociological Inquiry* 75, no. 4: 548–563.

Cobb, James C. 2005. *Away Down South: A History of Southern Identity.* New York: Oxford University Press.

Cohen, Dov, Joseph Vandello, Sylvia Puente, and Adrian Rantilla. 1999. "'When You Call Me That, Smile!' How Norms for Politeness, Interaction Styles, and Aggression Work Together in Southern Culture." *Social Psychology Quarterly* 62, no. 3: 257–275.

Collins, Patricia Hill. 1986. "Learning from the Outsider Within: The Sociological Significance of Black Feminist Thought." *Social Problems* 33, no. 6: 14–32.

———. 2004. *Black Sexual Politics: African Americans, Gender, and the New Racism*. New York: Routledge.

———. 2009. *Black Feminist Thought: Knowledge, Consciousness, and the Politics of Empowerment*. New York: Routledge.

Connell, Catherine. 2018. "Thank You for Coming Out Today: The Queer Discomforts in In-Depth Interviewing." In *Other, Please Specify: Queer Methods in Sociology*, edited by D'Lane Compton, Tey Meadow, and Kristen Schilt, 126–139. Palo Alto: University of California Press.

Connell, Raewyn. 2005. *Masculinities*. 2nd ed. California: University of California Press.

———. 2009. "Accountable Conduct: 'Doing Gender' in Transsexual and Political Retrospect." *Gender and Society* 23, no. 1: 104–111.

Connell, Raewyn, and James W. Messerschmidt. 2005. "Hegemonic Masculinity: Rethinking the Concept." *Gender and Society* 19, no. 6: 829–859.

Cragun, Ryan T., and J. E. Sumerau. 2015. "The Last Bastion of Sexual and Gender Prejudice? Sexualities, Race, Gender, Religiosity, and Spirituality in the Examination of Prejudice toward Sexual and Gender Minorities." *Journal of Sex Research* 52, no. 7: 821–834.

Curry, Tyler. 2014. "Why Gay Rights and Trans Rights Should Be Separated." *Huffington Post*, February 17, 2014. http://www.huffingtonpost.com/tyler-curry/gay-rights-and-trans-rights_b_4763380.html.

Daniel, Pete. 1996. *Standing at the Crossroads: Southern Life in the Twentieth Century*. Baltimore: John Hopkins University Press.

dickey, lore m., Stephanie L. Budge, Sabra L. Katz-Wise, and Michael V. Garza. 2016. "Health Disparities in the Transgender Community: Exploring Differences in Insurance Coverages." *Psychology of Sexual Orientation and Gender Diversity* 3, no. 3: 275–282.

Drysdale, Kerryn. 2019. *Intimate Investments in Drag King Cultures: The Rise and Fall of a Lesbian Social Scene*. Cham, Switzerland: Palgrave Macmillan.

Ezzell, Matthew B. 2012. "'I'm in Control': Compensatory Manhood in a Therapeutic Community." *Gender and Society* 26, no. 2: 190–215.

———. 2016. "Healthy for Whom?—Males, Men, and Masculinity: A Reflection on the Doing (and Study) of Dominance." In *Exploring Masculinities: Identity, Inequality, Continuity, and Change*, edited by C. J. Pascoe and Tristian Bridges, 188–197. New York: Oxford University Press.

Flores, Andrew R., Jody L. Herman, Gary J. Gates, and Taylor N. T. Brown. 2016. *How Many Adults Identify as Transgender in the United States?* Los Angeles: Williams Institute.

Freedom for All Americans. 2019. "Legislative Tracker: Anti-transgender Legislation." https://www.freedomforallamericans.org/2019-legislative-tracker/anti-transgender-legislation/.

Friend, Craig T. 2009. *Southern Masculinity: Perspectives on Manhood in the South since Reconstruction*. Athens: University of Georgia Press.

Friend, Craig Thompson, and Lorrie Glover. 2004. *Southern Manhood*. Athens: University of Georgia Press.

Galupo, M. Paz, Kyle S. Davis, Ashley L. Grynkiewicz, and Renae C. Mitchell. 2014. "Conceptualization of Sexual Orientation Identity among Sexual Minorities: Patterns across Sexual and Gender Identity." *Journal of Bisexuality* 14: 433–456.

GLADD. 2020. "Trump Accountability Project." Accessed October 23. https://www.glaad.org/tap/donald-trump.

Glenn, Evelyn Nakano. 2002. *Unequal Freedom: How Race and Gender Shaped American Citizenship and Labor*. Cambridge, MA: Harvard University Press.

Grady, James. 2019. "Making Their Own Way: Mac Huffington." *Out and About Nashville*. Accessed January 26, 2020. https://outandaboutnashville.com/making-their-own-way-mac-huffington/.

Grant, Jaime M., Lisa A. Mottet, Justin Tanis, Jack Harrison, Jody L. Herman, and Mara Keisling. 2011. *Injustice at Every Turn: A Report of the National Transgender Discrimination Survey*. National Center for Transgender Equality. Accessed January 1, 2019. http://www.transequality

.org/issues/resources/national-transgender-discrimination-survey-full-report.

Guadalupe-Diaz, Xavier L. 2019. *Transgressed: Intimate Partner Violence in Transgender Lives*. New York: New York University Press.

Halberstam, Jack. 1997. "Mackdaddy, Superfly, Rapper: Gender, Race, and Masculinity in the Drag King Scene." *Social Text* 52/53: 105–131.

———. 1998. *Female Masculinity*. Durham, NC: Duke University Press.

———. 1999. *The Drag King Book*. Photography by Del LaGrace Volcano. London: Serpent's Tail.

Howard, John. 1999. *Men Like That: A Southern Queer History*. Chicago: University of Chicago Press.

James, Sandy E., Jody L. Herman, Susan Rankin, Mara Keisling, Lisa Mottet, and Ma'ayan Anafi. 2016. *The Report of the 2015 U.S. Transgender Survey*. Washington, DC: National Center for Transgender Equality.

Johnson, Austin H. 2015. "Normative Accountability: How the Medical Model Influences Transgender Identities and Experiences." *Sociology Compass* 9, no. 9: 803–813.

———. 2016. "Transnormativity: A New Concept and Its Validation through Documentary Film about Transgender Men." *Sociological Inquiry* 86, no. 4: 465–491.

———. 2019. "Rejecting, Reframing, and Reintroducing: Trans People's Strategic Engagement with the Medicalisation of Gender Dysphoria." *Sociology of Health and Illness* 41, no. 3: 517–532.

Johnson, Austin H., Ivy Gibson-Hill, Jasmine Beach-Ferrara, Baker A. Rogers, and Andrew Bradford. 2020. "Common Barriers to Healthcare for Transgender People in the U.S. Southeast." *International Journal of Transgenderism* 21, no. 1: 70–78.

Johnson, Austin H., and Baker A. Rogers. 2019. "'We're the Normal Ones Here': Community Involvement, Peer Support, and Transgender Mental Health." *Sociological Inquiry* 90: 271–292.

Johnson, Colin R., Brian J. Gilley, and Mary L. Gray. 2016. Introduction to *Queering the Countryside: New Frontiers in Rural Queer Studies*, edited by Mary L. Gray, Colin R. Johnson, and Brian J. Gilley, 1–21. New York: New York University Press.

Johnson, E. Patrick. 2008. *Sweet Tea: Black Gay Men of the South*. Chapel Hill: University of North Carolina Press.

Kazyak, Emily. 2012. "Midwest or Lesbian? Gender, Rurality, and Sexuality." *Gender and Society* 26, no. 6: 825–848.

Kids Count Data Center. 2020. "Selected Kids Count Indicators for State in South Carolina." Annie E. Casey Foundation. Accessed May 17. https://datacenter.kidscount.org/data/customreports/42/7288,7246,43,5043,7244,5062,7247,7188,5116,5119,7245,7248,5425,7249,7243,7253,7250,106,5203,6795,7259.

Kosciw, Joseph G., Emily A. Greytak, and Elizabeth M. Diaz. 2009. "Who, What, Where, When, and Why: Demographic and Ecological Factors Contributing to Hostile School Climate for Lesbian, Gay, Bisexual, and Transgender Youth." *Journal of Youth and Adolescence* 38, no. 7: 976–988.

Lerner, Justin E., and Gabriel Robles. 2017. "Perceived Barriers and Facilitators to Health Care Utilization in the United States for Transgender People: A Review of Recent Literature." *Journal of Health Care for the Poor and Underserved* 28, no. 1: 127–152.

Lombardi, Emilia, Riki Wilchins, Dana Priesing, and Diana Malouf. 2001. "Gender Violence: Transgender Experiences with Violence and Discrimination." *Journal of Homosexuality* 42, no. 1: 89–101.

Mathers, Lain A. B. 2017. "Bathrooms, Boundaries, and Emotional Burdens: Cisgendering Interactions through the Interpretation of Transgender Experience." *Symbolic Interaction* 40, no. 3: 295–316.

Mathers, Lain A. B., J. E. Sumerau, and Ryan T. Cragun. 2018. "The Limits of Homonormativity Constructions of Bisexual and Transgender People in the Post-Gay Era." *Sociological Perspectives* 61, no. 6: 934–952.

Mayer, Kenneth H., Judith B. Bradford, Harvey J. Makadon, Ron Stall, Hillary Goldhammer, and Stewart Landers. 2008. "Sexual and Gender Minority Health: What We Know and What Needs to Be Done." *American Journal of Public Health* 98, no. 6: 989–995.

McDermott, Elizabeth, and Katrina Roen. 2012. "Youth on the Virtual Edge: Researching Marginalized Sexualities and Genders Online." *Qualitative Health Research* 22, no. 4: 560–570.

McInroy, Laruen B. 2016. "Pitfalls, Potentials, and Ethics of Online Survey Research: LGBTQ and Other Marginalized and Hard-to-Access Youths." *Social Work Research* 40, no. 2: 83–93.

McQueeney, Krista. 2009. "'We Are God's Children, Y'all': Race, Gender, and Sexuality in Lesbian- and Gay-Affirming Congregations." *Social Problems* 56, no. 1: 151–173.

Miller, Lisa R., and Eric Anthony Grollman. 2015. "The Social Costs of Gender Nonconformity for Transgender Adults: Implications for Discrimination and Health." *Sociological Forum* 30, no. 3: 809–831.

Miss Gay America. 2020. "About Miss Gay America." Accessed April 15. http://www.missgayamerica.com.

Mohanty, Chandra Talpade. 2003. *Feminism without Borders: Decolonizing Theory, Practicing Solidarity.* Durham, NC: Duke University Press.

Movement Advancement Project. 2020. "Georgia's Equality Profile." Accessed April 15. https://www.lgbtmap.org/equality_maps/profile_state/GA.

Nadal, Kevin, Avy Skolnick, and Yingloo Wong. 2012. "Interpersonal and Systemic Microaggressions toward Transgender People: Implications for Counseling." *Journal of LGBT Issues in Counseling* 11, no. 1: 55–82.

Newton, Esther. 1979. *Mother Camp: Female Impersonators in America.* Chicago: University of Chicago Press.

Noble, Jean Bobby. 2002. "Seeing Double, Thinking Twice: The Toronto Drag Kings and (Re-)Articulations of Masculinity." *Journal of Homosexuality* 43, no. 3–4: 251–261.

Orne, Jason. 2013. "Queers in the Line of Fire: Goffman's *Stigma* Revisited." *Sociological Quarterly* 54, no. 2: 229–253.

Pascoe, C. J., and Tristian Bridges, eds. 2016. *Exploring Masculinities: Identity, Inequality, Continuity, and Change.* New York: Oxford University Press.

Piontek, Thomas. 2002. "Kinging in the Heartland; or, The Power of Marginality." *Journal of Homosexuality* 43, no. 3–4: 125–143.

Reed, John Shelton. 1986. *The Enduring South.* Chapel Hill: University of North Carolina Press.

———. 2008. *Southerners: The Social Psychology of Sectionalism.* Institute for Research in Social Science Series. Charleston, SC: BookSurge.

———. 2018. *Mixing It Up: A South-Watcher's Miscellany.* Baton Rouge: Louisiana State University Press.

Reeves, Jackson. 2010. "Lena Lust Answers Our Questions." *Atlanta Magazine.* Accessed January 26, 2020. https://www.atlantamagazine.com/news-culture-articles/lena-lust-answers-our-questions/.

Roberts, Tangela S., Sharon G. Horne, and William T. Hoyt. 2015. "Between a Gay and a Straight Place: Bisexual Individuals' Experiences with Monosexism." *Journal of Bisexuality* 15, no. 4: 554–569.

Rodger, Gillian M. 2018. *Just One of the Boys: Female-to-Male Cross-Dressing on the American Variety Stage*. Champaign: University of Illinois Press.

Rogers, Baker A. 2018. "Drag as a Resource: Trans* and Nonbinary Individuals in the Southeastern United States." *Gender and Society* 32, no. 6: 889–910.

———. 2019. *Conditionally Accepted: Christians' Perspectives on Sexuality and Gay and Lesbian Civil Rights*. New Brunswick, NJ: Rutgers University Press.

———. 2020. *Trans Men in the South: Becoming Men*. Lanham, MD: Lexington Books.

Rupp, Lelia J., and Verta Taylor. 2003. *Drag Queens at the 801 Cabaret*. Chicago: University of Chicago Press.

Rupp, Lelia J., Verta Taylor, and Eve Ilana Shapiro. 2010. "Drag Queens and Drag Kings: The Difference Gender Makes." *Sexualities* 13, no. 3: 275–294.

Schilt, Kristen. 2006. "Just One of the Guys? How Transmen Make Gender Visible at Work." *Gender and Society* 20, no. 4: 465–490.

Schrock, Douglas, and Michael Schwalbe. 2009. "Men, Masculinity, and Manhood Acts." *Annual Review of Sociology* 35, no. 1: 277–295.

Senelick, Laurence. 2000. *The Changing Room: Sex, Drag and Theatre*. New York: Routledge.

Sennett, J., and Sarah Bay-Cheng. 2002. "'I Am the Man!' Performing Gender and Other Incongruities." *Journal of Homosexuality* 43, no. 3–4: 39–47.

Shapiro, Eve. 2007. "Drag Kinging and the Transformation of Gender Identities." *Gender and Society* 21, no. 2: 250–271.

Shields, Stephanie. 2008. "Gender: An Intersectionality Perspective." *Sex Roles* 59, no. 5: 301–311.

Shipherd, Jillian C., Kelly E. Green, and Sarah Abramovitz. 2010. "Transgender Clients: Identifying and Minimizing Barriers to Mental Health Treatment." *Journal of Gay and Lesbian Mental Health* 14, no. 2: 94–108.

Sinnard, Morgan T., Christopher R. Raines, and Stephanie L. Budge. 2016. "The Association between Geographic Location and Anxiety and Depression in Transgender Individuals: An Exploratory Study of an Online Sample." *Transgender Health* 1, no. 1: 181–186.

Smith, Erika W. 2019. "Ahead of the Met Gala, Remember: 'You Can't Have Camp without Queer.'" *Refinery29*. Accessed February 8, 2020. https://www.refinery29.com/en-us/2019/05/231016/camp-fashion-gay-culture-drag-lgbtq-history.

Smyth, Clare. 2008. *A Drag King Extravaganza* [Documentary]. San Francisco: Frameline.

Snorton, C. Riley. 2017. *Black on Both Sides: A Racial History of Trans Identity*. Minneapolis: University of Minnesota Press.

Sontag, Susan. 1964. "Notes on 'Camp.'" *Partisan Review* 31, no. 4: 515–530.

Stone, Amy L. 2018. "The Geography of Research on LGBTQ Life: Why Sociologists Should Study the South, Rural Queers, and Ordinary Cities." *Sociology Compass* 12, no. 11: 1–15.

Stroumsa, Daphna. 2014. "The State of Transgender Health Care: Policy, Law, and Medical Frameworks." *American Journal of Public Health* 104, no. 3: e31–e38.

Sue, Derald Wing. 2010. "Microaggressions, Marginality, and Oppression: An Introduction." In *Microaggressions and Marginality: Manifestation, Dynamics, and Impact*, edited by Derald Wing Sue. Hoboken, NJ: John Wiley and Sons.

Sumerau, J. E. 2012. "'That's What a Man Is Supposed to Do': Compensatory Manhood Acts in an LGBT Christian Church." *Gender and Society* 26, no. 3: 461–487.

Sumerau, J. E., and Ryan T. Cragun. 2018. *Christianity and the Limits of Minority Acceptance in America: God Loves (Almost) Everyone*. Lanham, MD: Lexington Books.

Sumerau, J. E., Eric Anthony Grollman, and Ryan T. Cragun. 2018. "'Oh My God, I Sound Like a Horrible Person': Generic Processes in the Conditional Acceptance of Sexual and Gender Diversity." *Symbolic Interaction* 42, no. 1: 62–82.

Testa, Rylan J., Crystal L. Jimenez, and Susan Rankin. 2014. "Risk and Resilience during Transgender Identity Development: The Effects of

Awareness and Engagement with Other Transgender People on Affect." *Journal of Gay and Lesbian Mental Health* 18, no. 1: 31–46.

Transgender Law Center. 2020. "Equality Maps." Accessed June 17. https://transgenderlawcenter.org/equalitymap.

Troka, Donna, Kathleen Lebesco, and Jean Noble, eds. 2002. *The Drag King Anthology*. New York: Haworth Press.

USofA. 2020. "History—USofA Pageants LLC." Accessed May 1. https://usofa.org/history/.

Ward, Jane. 2018. "The Methods Gatekeepers and the Exiled Queers." In *Other, Please Specify: Queer Methods in Sociology*, edited by D'Lane Compton, Tey Meadow, and Kristen Schilt, 51–66. Palo Alto: University of California Press.

Ward, Robbie. 2013. "Mississippi Town Sued after Refusing to License Gay Bar." Reuters. Accessed January 26, 2020. https://www.reuters.com/article/us-usa-gaybar-lawsuit/mississippi-town-sued-after-refusing-to-license-gay-bar-idUSBRE99015Y20131001.

Watts, Trent, ed. 2008. *White Masculinity in the Recent South*. Baton Rouge: Louisiana State University Press.

West, Candace, and Don H. Zimmerman. 1987. "Doing Gender." *Gender and Society* 1, no. 2: 125–151.

———. 2009. "Accounting for Doing Gender." *Gender and Society* 23, no. 1: 11–22.

Weston, Kath. 1997. *Families We Choose: Gays, Lesbians, Kinship*. New York: Columbia University Press.

Willox, Annabelle. 2002. "Whose Drag Is It Anyway? Drag Kings and Monarchy in the UK." *Journal of Homosexuality* 43, no. 3–4: 263–284.

Wilson, Lena. 2020. "Where Did All the Lesbian Bars Go? Increasingly, They're on TV." *New York Times*, May 7. https://www.nytimes.com/2020/05/07/arts/television/lesbian-bars-vida-l-word-batwoman.html.

Wong, Kristen. 2019. "The Curious Disappearance of the Lesbian Bar." Accessed May 31, 2020. https://thestoryexchange.org/the-curious-disappearance-of-the-lesbian-bar/.

Index

About the Author

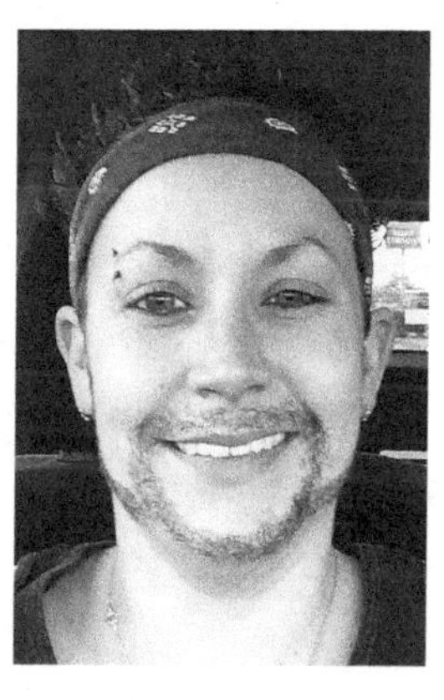

BAKER A. ROGERS is an associate professor of sociology at Georgia Southern University. They hold a PhD in sociology from Mississippi State University and a master of social work from Winthrop University. Their research focuses on inequality, specifically examining the intersections of gender, sexuality, and religion in the southeastern United States. They have two previously published books, *Conditionally Accepted: Christians' Perspectives on Sexuality and Gay and Lesbian Civil Rights* and *Trans Men in the South: Becoming Men*. Baker's academic articles are published in *Gender and Society*, *Men and Masculinities*, *Journal of Interpersonal Violence*, *Qualitative Sociology*, *Sociological Spectrum*, *Sociological Inquiry*, *International Journal of Transgenderism*, *Sexualities*, *Review of Religious Research*, *International Journal of Social Research Methodology*, and *Feminist Teacher*.

About the Author